I humbly and respectfully

dedicate this work to

Martin Burns,

Frank Gotch,

Ed Lewis,

Lou Thesz,

Karl Gotch,

Gene LeBell,

Tony Cecchine

and Kory Hays

— past, present and future

masters of the fine sport

and art.

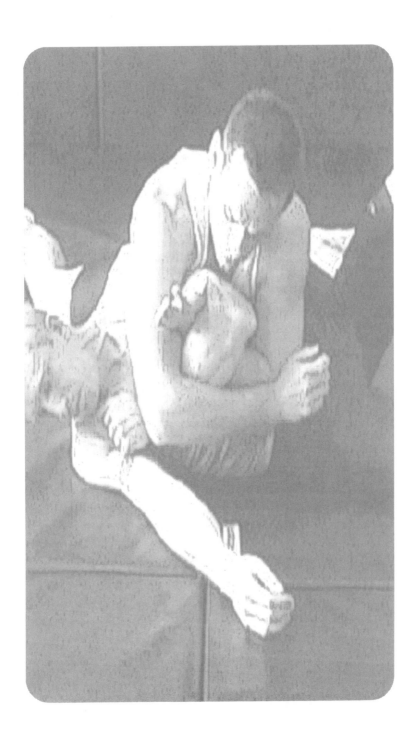

More No Holds Barred Fighting
Killer Submissions

Mark Hatmaker
Doug Werner

Tracks Publishing
San Diego, California

TRACKS
PUBLISHING

More No Holds Barred Fighting

Killer Submissions

Mark Hatmaker / Doug Werner

Tracks Publishing
140 Brightwood Avenue
Chula Vista, CA 91910
619-476-7125
trkspub@pacbell.net
www.startupsports.com

Copyright © 2003 by Doug Werner
2nd printing 11-05

Publisher's Cataloging-in-Publication

Hatmaker, Mark.
    More no holds barred fighting : killer submissions /
Mark Hatmaker, Doug Werner.
    p. cm.
    Includes index.
    LCCN 2003105216
    ISBN 1884654185

    1. Wrestling.   I. Werner, Doug, 1950-   II. Title.

GV1195.H375 2003   796.8'123
                          QBI03-200367

Acknowledgements

Aisha Buxton for graphic production.

Phyllis Carter for her mighty red pen.

Greg D'Amico for the generous use of his gym.

Kylie Hatmaker for her unwavering support.

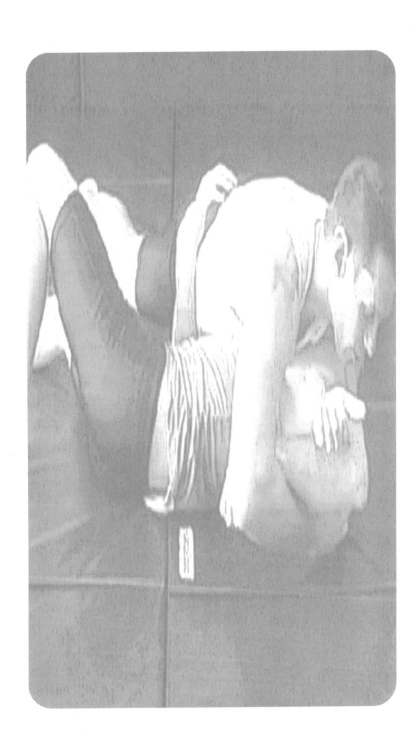

Preface

Welcome to *Killer Submissions!*

Man, it feels good to write that title. It feels so good that I'm going to write it again. Welcome to *Killer Submissions!* Why am I so excited about it? For the same reason you are. Ninety percent of this book is about tapping the opposition out. Come on, let's face it, that's why we got into this sport in the first place — we wanted in on the beauty of hitting our opponent with things he has never seen before. Don't get me wrong, striking is fantastic and it is indeed a science unto itself, but it is also the aspect of the game where a big strong guy can throw a lucky shot and snag the KO. There is NO way that anyone can hit a lucky double-wrist lock or a lucky refined sleeper. No, that takes science. Submissions are about positioning, control and leverage — three components that don't happen by chance.

When I wrote *No Holds Barred Fighting: The Ultimate Guide to Submission Wrestling,* my goal was to bring all the basic ideas, concepts and techniques necessary to send the athlete down an intelligent path to mastery of the sport all wrapped up in an economical package. I love that book. I feel that all of the information found in it is of great value, and I heartily hope that you have studied it well before running through this little cookbook and putting your own painful stews together. I sincerely believe that you can know all of the submissions in the world, but if you can't wrestle (I mean *real* wrestling: controlling, riding and pressuring) you won't rise to the top of your ability. As much as I love that book, the book you now hold was in the back of my mind while writing the first — that is, a compact, transportable submission guide. I wanted to fill the first text with many more hooks, submissions, uncle-inducers, whatever you want to call them, but I knew that it was and is vital to provide the essential groundwork (no pun intended) to get you going.

To truly capture the full panoply of the NHB game, there needs to be an accompanying text on NHB striking and NHB conditioning (trust me, they are already in the works). I gave you the basics in *No Holds Barred Fighting*. With *Killer Submissions* you've got the first of many references for tapping (submissions are seemingly endless). One problem in writing this volume was not how to fill it but what to leave out. For the most part, this book is pure OD taps.

Now a few things about how this cookbook is put together:

1. If you are already a skilled player, and thumbing through you find a move you think you already know, please take the time to read the description to see if there are any little tweaks that might add to you current technique.

2. Some submissions will be shown in isolation, that is, in a *Hey, here's a neat move* manner. These isolated moves are usually bread-and-butter techniques that can be applied in many positions so we offer them in their easiest view for learning.

3. Most submissions will be offered in chain fashion in

which we link one submission to another and to another and so on. This is done to inculcate a logical call and response pattern that follows your opponent's likely attempted counters. I firmly believe that learning submissions in pragmatic chains as opposed to a random *Hey, have you seen this one?* fashion contributes to faster development as an intelligent fighter.

4. Please do not ignore the chapter on breath control. I consider this component of the game to be integral to your success.

5. If you already have the basics down as presented in the first volume you can bounce around this book as your taste dictates. Where the first book was meant to be consumed straight through, this one can be started anywhere or at the beginning. The choice is yours.

With all that said, let's open the cookbook, select a recipe and let your opponent feel how it tastes to be on the receiving end.

Have fun and train safely,

Mark Hatmaker

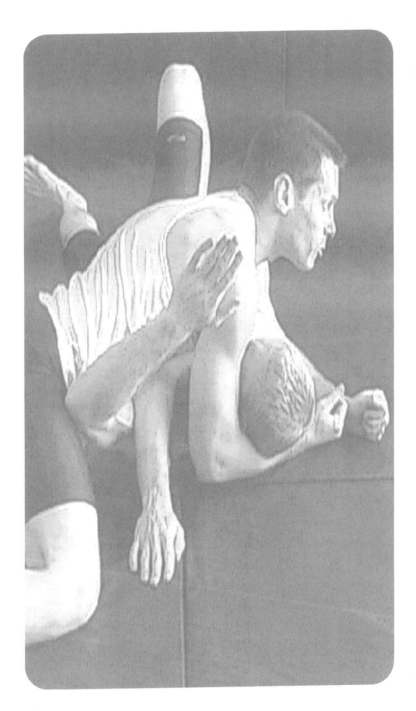

Contents

> **Warning label**
> Submission wrestling includes contact and can be dangerous. Use proper equipment and train safely. Practice with restraint and respect for your partners. Drill for fun, fitness and to improve skills. Do not fight with the intent to do harm.

Training principles

Key points you should strive to keep in mind before beginning any conditioning program or formulating one for yourself:

Specificity
Training should transfer favorably to specific sport.

Synergism
Training should be scheduled in sequences to allow greatest development.

Somatotrophics / body weight resistance
Training should build ability to control body weight through all ranges of motion.

Efficiency
Training should get the job done economically regarding time consumed.

Effectiveness
Training should get the job done in a manner that ensures that the right job is getting done.

Reality maintenance
Training should allow time to live life, work your job and enjoy your family.

1 Conditioning

Sound strategy

Mixed martial artists and combat athletes have always been concerned with training for optimum results. Boxing rings, cages and wrestling mats are harsh venues. Less than optimum training methods reap less than stellar results. The arguments in conditioning are usually those of exercise choices:

Do I lift weights?

Do I work only with my body weight?

Do I cycle?

Do I run stairs?

I won't even pretend to propose an optimum conditioning program (we'll cover that in its entirety in another volume). What I do intend is to spotlight specific principles that you should strive to keep in mind before beginning any conditioning program or formulating one for yourself.

Specificity

The first principle is that of specificity. Specificity refers to patterns of physical movement, physical demands and even comparative environments that transfer favorably to the sport you have chosen to better. For example, if you wish to be a better golfer, it is *not* necessary to spend two hours in the weight room four days a week or to perform sets of wind sprints. There is no doubt that your condition for these specific activities (weightlifting and wind sprints) would improve, but there would be little if any progress made in your golf game. To improve your game it is advisable to spend more time on the golf course driving, chipping and putting. In other words, you should select a regimen that is specific to your goal.

The same holds true for combat athletes. You must examine every training modality that comes your way to see if it does indeed have any transfers to what your sport is all about. For example, we all know that endurance is required for NHB, but what kind of endurance? The kind found in marathon runners? In speed skaters? In cross-country skiing? The answer is you need the kind of endurance found in NHB athletes. Sports kinesiologists have known for some time that the conditioning demands of one sport are poorly transferred to another. This view was expressed succinctly by UFC veteran Pedro Rizzo who said, *"Runners run, swimmers swim, fighters fight."*

So, to speak in general terms, the kind of endurance found in NHB would not be that of the Long Slow Distance (LSD) variety associated with long distance running. Logging lots of miles may be detrimental to your training if the fight game is your primary goal. NHB requires more from your anaerobic capacity than it does from your aerobic capacity. Thus your search for supplemental endurance work should be more of the anaerobic variety. Furthermore, that anaerobic training should be comprised of movements that parallel those of your endeavor or better yet be comprised of those actual movements.

Synergism
The next principle to keep in mind while assembling your conditioning toolbox is that of synergy. It is not enough to choose exercises for their specific transfers. It is advisable to stack the regimen in sequences that will allow for greater development. For example, your workout may be comprised of some heavy anaerobic work that will tax your fine motor skills to a particular degree, and yet you intend on working pinpoint combination punching. It would be wise to order your fine motor skill work before any severely taxing work so that you are in possession of all of your resources. You can return to punching after your anaerobic work (good punching drills may actually comprise your anaerobic work), but these punches performed once taxed are more for continued anaerobic and muscular endurance to mimic the later stages of the fight than to fix neuromuscular grooves.

Another example of efficient synergistic stacking is found in our *Gladiator Conditioning* material. We recommend a pulling group, which is a series of pull-ups, and a grip group, a series of exercises designed to improve grip endurance. To stack them synergistically, we work our grip *after* the pulling group to prevent our fatigued grip from interfering with the possible gains in the pulling group. It is wise to examine your routine for synergistic stacking. Make sure that one exercise is not interfering with gains in another.

Somatotrophics
This term refers to body-weight resistance work. I am going to take myself out of the line of fire in the debate of weights versus body-weight conditioning. There is plenty of evidence on both sides to make convincing cases for each, although much of the evidence that is cited seems to be of the anecdotal variety and thus precludes its serious consideration in the schism. From a middle ground position I think it is safe to say that the ground floor of your conditioning structure should be the ability to control your own body weight through all ranges of motion. By control, I mean possessing the muscular strength and endurance, as applied through simple calisthenics, to maneuver your body freely in manners similar to your athletic endeavor. Without good control of your own body, it is a stretch to believe that the combat athlete will find within his grasp some of the more advanced combinations and chains that require precise kinesthetic control in all ranges.

With that stated as an argument for a base in body-weight exercises as a foundation for building such control, I see nothing that prohibits the addition of weightlifting to increase the functional strength of the combat athlete. Just be sure that any weight exercise passes the tests for specificity and synergy before its inclusion. Keep in mind that a good argument can be made for simply adding a weight vest and ankle and wrist weights to the somatotrophic base to increase the resistance gradually (in the Milo of Crotona manner) while still essentially performing exercises closer to specific applications.

Efficiency and effectiveness
Efficiency can be defined as getting the job done in an economical manner regarding time consumed. Effectiveness can be defined as getting the job done in a manner that ensures that the right job is getting done. To put these definitions into stark relief, a workout that consists of nothing but crunches and takes only 20 minutes is time efficient. But is it effective for the combat fighter? Of course not. Too many factors would be ignored. Where's the aerobic and anaerobic work? The total body flexibility program? Overall muscular strength and endurance work? On the other hand, a workout consisting of 300 exercises to develop punching power, speed, and endurance is highly effective but the amount of time needed to complete such a regimen is far from efficient.

A good workout will blend the aspects of efficiency and effectiveness so that each exercise is chosen for its effective specific transfers and chosen carefully to not take an exorbitant amount of time. An optimum conditioning regimen is intense, specific and of short duration.

The short duration is vital on two counts. First, the more efficient and effective your workout the more time you have to devote to actual fight training as opposed to just logging longer conditioning hours. Second, by training in a time efficient manner, you are more likely to pursue such a regimen since it does not seem as daunting in time consumption and it will leave you with enough free time for reality maintenance. By reality maintenance I mean enough time to live your life, work your job and see your family. Many workouts exist on paper as very nice wishes, but do not consider the demands of the non-sponsored, non-endorsed, has-a-day-job, everyday athlete.

Conclusion

There you have it. To devise an optimum conditioning routine that takes into account all of the above considerations, you must test it for specificity, synergy, baseline body control through somatotrophics, efficiency and effectiveness, and measure it all against reality maintenance. Without careful consideration of the above, I have sincere doubts that your time will be used to its optimum. Keeping this in mind I believe you now have the strategic components to approach many regimens and to judge them according to your own needs.

Remember this is only a strategic approach to evaluating regimens. It will take another volume to cover the specifics of an optimum routine that would include technique cultivation, muscular strength and endurance work, aerobic and anaerobic work, plyometric work, speed mechanics, agility work, cognitive work, scheduled rests and breaks, total body flexibility and nutritional intake. The only aspect not mentioned in that list is breath work, and I consider that component so important that we will cover it in this volume. It's next.

2 Take a breather

The ultimate importance of breath control

What's a chapter on breath work doing in a book on hardcore NHB fighting? It seems more appropriate to find it in a New Age or alternative health tome. Well, hold on to your hats because I'm here to tell you that breath work is perhaps *the* foundation on which successful mat work is built. Good breath work is fundamental to all athletic endeavors, but it seems to lend itself particularly well to mat work where partner compressions (i.e., heavy guy laying on your chest) can make normal patterns impossible.

Breath work is integral to your game since it is the only component of the autonomic nervous system that falls under our control. Heart and digestion rates are out of our hands beyond their eventual shifts through conditioning, but your respiration can be controlled and directed. You can learn to choose the rate of your respiration, the depth of intake, the rate of outtake, force of exhalation and even direct your breathing to different lung areas.

Why would the control of such functions be of interest to the NHB athlete? We know that the body is fueled by your nutritional intake (that you have control of and can modify), your liquid intake (again, under your power) and that you are also fueled in the psychodynamic arena through thoughts, attitudes and anxieties regarding your athletic performance (again under your control although maybe a bit tougher to regulate than the physical concerns). Your respiration fuels all of these processes. There is no fuel process that can be metabolized in the body without the presence of oxygen.

Oxygen is brought into the body by the lungs and distributed throughout the body by oxygenated blood. The lungs release depleted gases (carbon dioxide) on exhalation. So if all fuel functions can only take place in the presence of oxygen and oxygenated blood, it stands to reason that the base fuel process is that of respiration. After all, one can go for weeks without food and days without water but only a few minutes without oxygen.

By acknowledging that respiration is the core fuel process and gaining an understanding of how we can control its different characteristics, we can economize and energize our primary fuel usage.

Competing breath rates
Most people inexperienced in a particular athletic
endeavor have a tendency to hold their breath during
exertion or at the very least use inefficient breathing
patterns. By doing so they greatly reduce their overall
performance and endurance. A simple strategy I use
when rolling is that of competing or comparative
breath rates. Mat work is ideal for this strategy as the
proximity of competitors allows one to hear what the
other person is doing. To take advantage of this
strategy, merely listen to the breath rate of your partner
during a roll and attempt to bring your rate in under
his. It's as easy as calming your rate and lengthening
the intake and outtake of your breath. By doing so you
will more fully oxygenate your blood, calm your mind
and body, and reduce any excess tension or struggling
in a game that is primarily about leverage. Slower and
deeper breath rates will outlast fast and shallow rates
every time.

Clearing breath
The idea of breath control sounds fine in the theoret-
ical sense, but practical application in a sport that goes
into anaerobic areas makes it tough to downright
impossible to maintain a controlled rate. Scrambled
bursts that redline into anaerobic areas cause you to
gasp for air once you come out of the anaerobic redline. The reason for the hyperventilation is found in the
name itself, anaerobic, which means without oxygen.
The scrambled activity happens so fast that present
oxygen reserves get exhausted, and the activity continues at a rate faster than new oxygen intake can keep
up with. Once you come out of this redline your lungs
will naturally pump at a faster rate trying to rectify this

depleted state. The problem is that your faster rate is not allowing for maximum exhalation before your next inhalation and waste gases (carbon dioxide) are still cycled within the lungs. They are taking up space and not allowing for a full oxygen intake — keeping you on the hyperventilation cycle — attempting to burn fuel where there really is none to be burned.

To pull yourself out of this cycle, all you have to do is the opposite of your natural instincts. Instead of gasping for air, forcefully exhale *all* of the contents of your lungs in a long audible breath (a sort of whooshing sound). Once all waste gases have been expelled by the clearing breath, your next breath will be a long controlled full breath of energizing oxygen. From there return to comparative/competitive breathing.

Energizing breath
This is a specialized pattern for use when energy reserves are low. You are in the late stages of the match and you feel sluggish (usually due to poor removal of waste products throughout the body). The energizing breath is a quick pick-me-up to access your core fuel source. You essentially hyperventilate at an extremely fast rate, two to four inhalation/exhalation cycles per second, using shallow breaths. This rapid pattern need be done for only 15 to 20 seconds to forcefully reintroduce your core fuel. Try this not only in your training but in your everyday life when sluggishness sets in. It can provide an extra temporary boost.

Sidenote
It is advisable to make all of your breathing patterns audible. By inhaling and exhaling in audible whooshes, the sound itself can act as a mnemonic device to remind you to concentrate on your breath control first and foremost. The audible pattern also helps provide mental focus. And lastly, the audible pattern has been known to be a bit disconcerting to unseasoned rolling partners and can be just one more weapon in your arsenal.

Compressed breath
There will be times when your chest will be compressed by your opponent or you will be stacked in unnatural positions. It is in these compressed positions that extreme diligence must be paid to breath control. When placed into one of these positions, you must focus on keeping your rate under control. You've got to learn to relax in what are decidedly unrelaxing positions. In these positions you will not have access to your entire lung surface area. By relaxing your breath you can learn to make the most of the surface area you do have access to.

To train this contingency outside of actual partner rolling compression, grab a heavy bag and lay it on the mat. Lie cross-body on the bag placing your diaphragm against the bag. Stay off your knees and arch your diaphragm into the bag. The only points of contact will be your toes into the mat and your diaphragm being pressed into the bag. Hold this position for three minutes. Performing this exercise will allow you to relax your breathing even when you have less than full lung access.

For extra stress, try performing a series of jump squats and then moving immediately into this exercise to duplicate the higher breath rates that scrambles induce.

Stacked breath
This is a companion exercise to the compressed breath. Here again we are dealing with less than optimal lung coverage. Lie on the mat and roll your legs over your shoulders in imitation of a stacked position — in yogic parlance, a plough posture. Compact your stack as extreme as you can tolerate and hold for three minutes while you learn to breath in this shallow lung position.

Try performing the same exercise after a series of jump squats as stated in the previous pattern to learn to control the breath after a scramble. These two exercises are of significant value as they adhere to the specificity principle in conditioning.

Relaxing breath

This pattern is meant to be performed before or after your rolling session. It is meant to educate filling the lungs to full capacity, holding the breath in an anaerobic state and then conditioning the diaphragmatic musculature to assist in full expulsion. It is also useful for calming prematch jitters and can be used in your daily life in addition to your NHB training.

To perform the relaxing breath you do nothing more than adhere to the following ratio: 4-7-8. In other words, inhale to full capacity at a slow 4 count, hold your breath at full capacity for a 7 count, and then slowly, fully exhale at a slow 8 count. Perform a minimum of ten cycles of this repeating ratio for full benefit.

That's it. Breath control strategy, physiology and five patterns to assist you in your progress in the sport. Remember, breath control is as vital as technique and it is advisable to make it a regular part of your training. As a matter of fact, there should be no aspect of your training where you are not aware of your breath rate and its quality. This sort of attention to your core fuel source will accelerate your rate of learning appreciably.

Take a breather

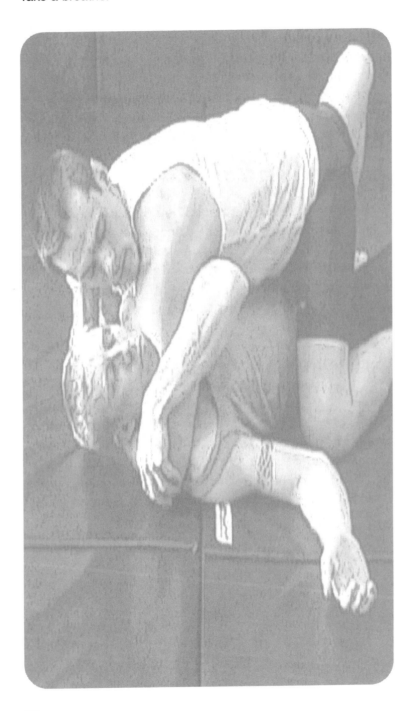

3 Take it to heart

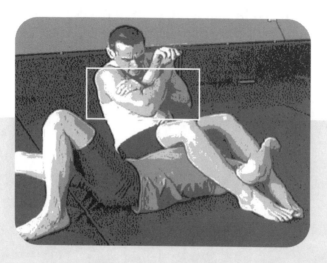

One more thing before we get rolling.

I want you to "take it to heart" in regards to the coaching tip I'm about to offer. Your body is at its strongest as it draws in toward its center. In other words, all motions pulling into your center of mass are stronger than those pulling away from your center of mass.

Example:
Hold a medicine ball tightly to your chest and ask a partner to pull it away. Try it again while you hold the ball away from your chest. You should find that you are strongest when tucking the ball tightly toward your heart and retaining it with your arms (elbows tucked tight to your sides).

Remember the results of this experiment when retaining any hold whether it be a pin, ride or submission. Focus on bringing the desired portion of your opponent's anatomy into your heart.

4 Killer submission chains

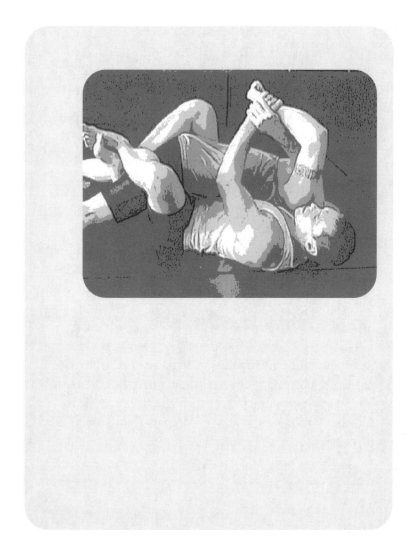

4.1 Scarlet Pimpernel series (beating the guillotine)

This chain runs through all the necessary steps needed to beat the standard guillotine choke as we know it. The guillotine is a go-to move for most players but, to be quite frank, you have very little to fear from it once you run this series a hundred or so times. It is vitally impor- tant to have this entire series down as this go-to is usually snagged as you shoot your double-leg takedown. Now you don't want to give up your double-leg since it's a *very* high percentage drop, so let's make sure that you can blow through these reversals just as quickly as you shoot. You should think of these reversals as a necessary part of the double-leg and not just as *uh-oh* moves.

Go-behind

● Once caught, turn to face the crook of his elbow.

● Pull down on his hands with your inside hand.

● Drop your base and step toward his back with your outside foot.

● As you step behind and drop your base, snap the back of your head out and up to release. Important — You must pull out with the back of your head leading. Leading with the side of your head will strain your neck.

● Gain your opponent's back.

Another view ...

Assisted lift slam

● The assistance is provided by your opponent placing your head under his arm.
● Here the grip is so snug that the turn to the crook of the arm is stopped.
● Grab his far hip with your inside hand.
● Underhook his crotch with the crook of your outside arm.
● Step into him and back lift him from the mat.
● Slam him to the mat following him to cover (next page).

Assisted elevator

● Your opponent has sagged his hips away from you preventing both the go-behind and the penetration necessary for the assisted lift.
● Post both of your hands on his hips.

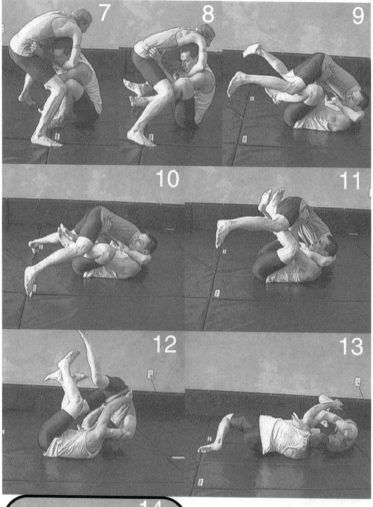

● Sit underneath him and place your insteps under his thighs.

● Arch your back toward your free side and kick your feet toward the sky to bring him over the top.

● If he persists in his hold, he will assist in bringing you to top saddle/mount position.

Sprawled inside legs guillotine beat to double wrist lock off the back

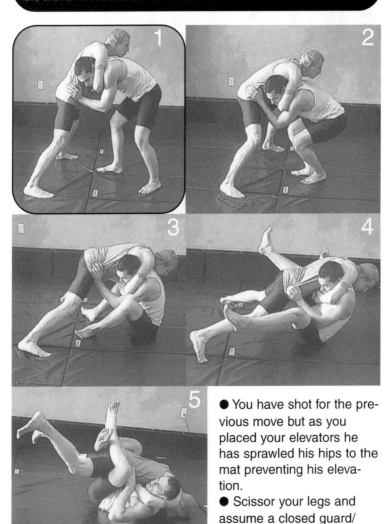

● You have shot for the previous move but as you placed your elevators he has sprawled his hips to the mat preventing his elevation.

● Scissor your legs and assume a closed guard/ bottom scissors position.

● Grab his attacking wrist with your outside hand (here your left).

● Pass your inside arm (here your right arm) over the top of his head to bring your arm between your heads.

● Arch your back hard as you push away with your scissored legs, pull on his hand with your left hand and push his head away with your draped right arm.

● As he releases his grip, maintain your hold on his hand, remove your head and secure a double wrist lock by figure-4ing your hands and traveling his arm in an outside arc toward his head to tap.

Guillotine guard drop — the spear

● Your opponent secures his guillotine and then drops to his back placing you in a bottom scissors/guard position.

● Immediately grab his attacking wrist with your outside hand (here your left) and pull toward his hip to loosen his grip.
● Place the fingers of your inside hand (your right) into his jugular notch (the groove of bone at the top of the sternum). If this is not permitted in your competition rules, place the point of your outside elbow (right elbow) into his sternum or solar plexus and stack through your placement point for your release.

Suplex (assisted takedown option) to northern lights to cross-body double wrist lock

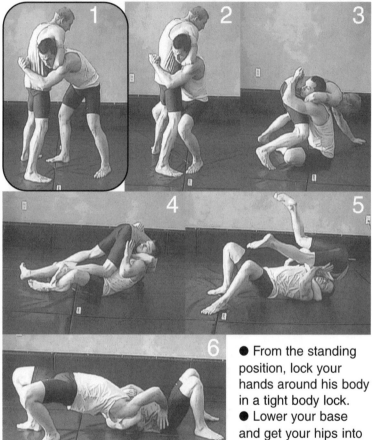

● From the standing position, lock your hands around his body in a tight body lock.
● Lower your base and get your hips into him and hit a tight back arch.
● As soon as you hit a back neck bridge position, post your hands on his hips and (next page) kick over to a top saddle/mount position. The hands in the hips prevents you from being caught in a full or half guard. If you are caught, just hit the release described in the guillotine guard drop.

● Transition from the top saddle/mount to hit a cross-body ride on the side opposite your head (here moving to your right).

● Grab his attacking hand with your hip-side hand and drive it to the mat pulling your head out as you do.

● Underhook his right upper arm with your right arm and lock your hands in a figure-4 grip.

● Pull your elbows tight to his body.

● Squeeze your elbows together and arch your chest through him to tap.

Arm drape

Caution — Do not use this technique

● The arm drape is a very common stalemate or preparatory move for many other guillotine releases.
● The inside arm is placed either over the opponent's open shoulder or the shoulder nearest his lock.
● The theory is that this removes his leverage for the guillotine and allows you survival time or the chance to run to a backstep.
● Take a look at the following arm drape counter to understand why we do not advocate.

⟶

Guillotine backstep

● I do not advocate the use of the standard guillotine but rather the figure-4 and chancery series, which were described in our first book.

● If you do use the guillotine, use the following steps whether or not he hits the arm drape. It works with or without, the drape just makes it *much* easier.

● Release your locking wrist with your inside hand and reach across his back to clutch his lat. (Here you are reaching across his back with your left hand.)

● Backstep with your foot on your guillotine side and take him to the mat (backstep with your right).

● Cover him with a cross-body while retaining your hold on his head.

● Cinch your grip around his head and arch over your head-side shoulder to tap.

4.2 Turn the corner series

Top body top wrist lock

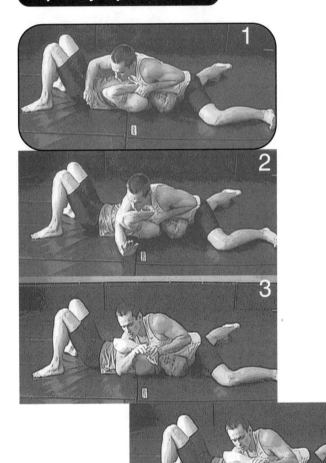

● From a tight top body ride, hook underneath your opponent's left elbow with the crook of your right arm.

● Grab his left hand with your left hand. Be sure to grab his hand with your thumb to the inside of his palm and your fingers grasping the back of his hand.

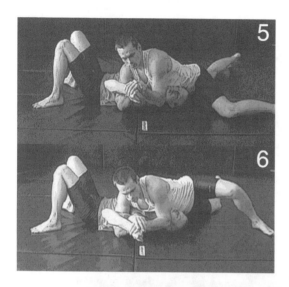

● Use your elbows to jones him (drive your elbows through his face and/or sternum to tenderize him a bit).

● Using not just your left arm but your entire body weight, drive his left arm to the mat.

● Secure a figure-4 grip on his arm.

● Sit out on your right hip driving his head toward his left shoulder.

● Drag your elbows into his body, squeeze them together and twist his hand with your left to tap.

Turned short arm scissors (SAS)

Your opponent has resisted your attempts to drive his arm to the mat in the previous move (or in all likelihood you have chosen to jones too politely).

● Replace the crook of your right arm with the crook of your left arm.

● Grab his left hand with your right hand this time. Grab it with your palm facing up with your thumb on top.

● Keeping your hips low (as always), turn the corner to your left as if shifting to a cross-body ride.

● As you shift to this position, grip your hands into a figure-4 grip.

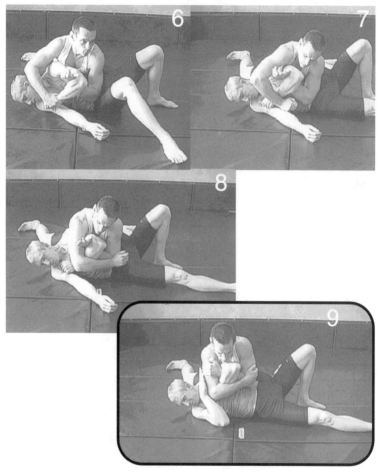

● Stay low and use your upper chest to pressure him onto his right side.

● Drive the inner cutting edge of your left forearm tight into the crook of his left arm. You do this by pointing your thumb toward the crook of his arm and wedging deeply. Be sure to stay with bone wedged in and not the soft meat of your forearm.

● Hook the crook of your right arm over his left wrist as close to the end of his arm as you can manage without losing his arm.

● Grip your triceps with your hands, squeeze your elbows together and arch your chest through his arm to tap.

Dragging down arm bar

● Your opponent has resisted your SAS so you reclasp your figure-4 grip.
● Run your hips around the top of his head while staying heavy. You do this by using your left armpit as a pivot point on his left armpit as you travel around never allowing your hips or knees to hit the mat.

● Once you pass the top of his head on your travel, sit out onto your left hip (figure of speech really — never allow your hip to make contact with the mat, it relieves too much pressure off your opponent) while dragging his arm with you. Think of sliding into home plate.

● Maintaining your figure-4 grip, straighten his arm and arch your left armpit into his elbow to tap.

Slammed home double wrist lock

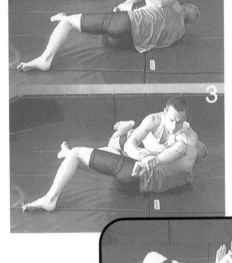

● You can hit this as a counter for your opponent's resistance against the previous move or you can bypass it and run directly to the slammed double for a hard-hitting move in and of itself.

● Maintaining your figure-4 grip on his left arm and your pressure on his body, turn toward his hips for a cross-body ride.

● Drive his left arm to the mat on his left side.

● Drag your elbows into his body, squeeze them together and twist his hand to tap.

Chasing short arm scissors (SAS)

● Your opponent has straightened his arm against your slammed double wrist lock.

● You will essentially hit movement #2 from this series.

● Point your left thumb toward the crook of his left arm and wedge your wrist deep. Remember — Use the bony area of your wrist and not the meat.

● Overhook his left wrist with the crook of your right arm.

● Grip your triceps, squeeze your elbows together and arch your chest through his arm to tap.

4.3 Double cross-face series

cross-face crank

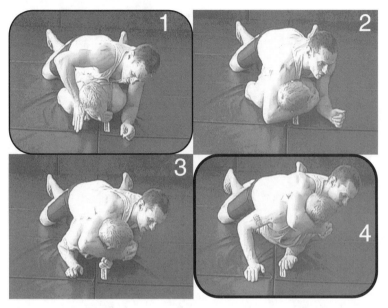

● Your opponent is belly down and you have opted to ride him with no hooks (not a bad idea, by the way).

● Hit a standard cross-face with your right arm by entering your hand at the jaw line on the right side of his face and then forcing the inner edge of your forearm across his face directly underneath his nose.

● Grip his left triceps with your right hand.

● Place your left hand on the left upper quadrant of his head.

● Push down on his head with your left hand while levering his chin over his left shoulder to tap.

Double cross crank

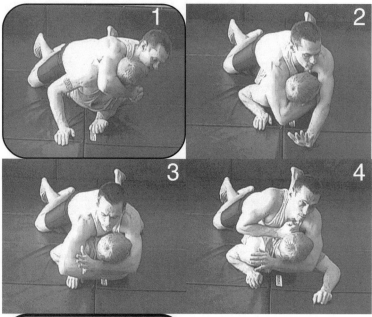

● Your opponent is resisting your cross-face crank.
● From cross-face position run your left arm under his head from your left side. Important — Leave him facing his left as he has been forced to do by your initial cross-face.

● Wedge his face tight to the crook of your left arm.
● Remove your cross-facing right arm and run it behind his back and place your right hammer fist on top of his left scapula. When levering off the back with your arms always use the hammer fist position — it's a harder lever.
● Use the crook of your left arm to turn his chin toward his left shoulder while pushing down on his left scapula with your right hammer fist to tap.

Double cross-face turnover

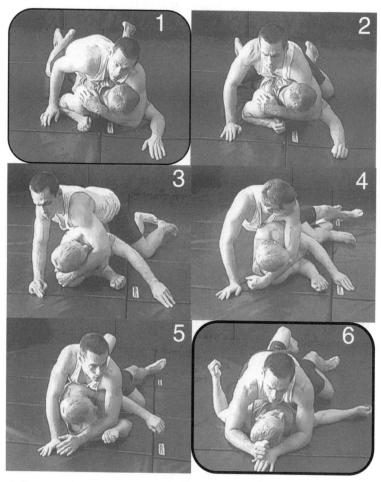

- Your opponent has resisted your double cross crank.
- Leave your double cross-face in place.
- Remove your right hand from his scapula.
- Give him some space to turn by opening your right leg a bit.
- Turn him on his back by using the crook of your left arm to make him look over his left shoulder.
- Secure the top saddle /mount position.

4.4 Two hooks for thought and one to avoid and why

Chest press neck crank

● You've turned him into the top saddle position. Now it's time to hit some natural follow-up hooks.

● Hit a double grapevine.

● Run your left arm around the back of his neck with your thumb pointing up.

● Run your right forearm behind the back of his neck with thumb pointing up.

● Stack your forearms on top of one another.

● Position your upper chest so that his chin is tight against it.

● Stretch his lower body away with your grapevines while arching your chest through his chin over your forearms to tap.

Pop to cross-body scoop hook

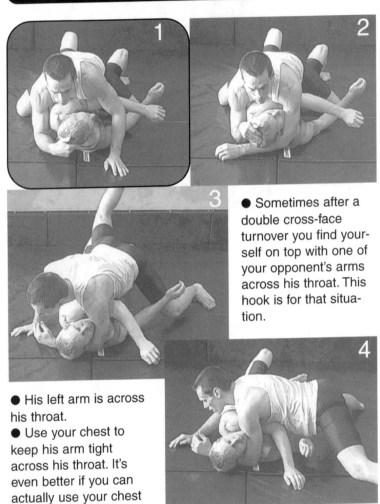

● Sometimes after a double cross-face turnover you find yourself on top with one of your opponent's arms across his throat. This hook is for that situation.

● His left arm is across his throat.
● Use your chest to keep his arm tight across his throat. It's even better if you can actually use your chest and move it further down his body.
● Run your left arm behind his neck as in the previous move.
● Pop your hips over to a right cross-body ride keeping your left arm behind his neck and keeping the pressure through his chest so that he can't free his left arm. It is important that you keep him flat on his back and not allow him to turn toward you on the pop over. Not a problem if you practice good pressure in all of your wrestling.

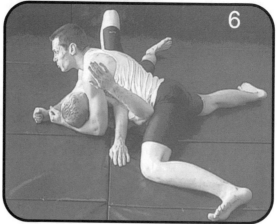

● Shove your left shoulder tight into his face and tap either of two ways:
1. Use your free right hand to reach over and grab the right side of his head and pull it to his left shoulder or
2. Using your chest to keep his arm wedged *tight* between your bodies, use the crook of your left arm to hit him above the ear line on the right side of his head to move his head toward his left shoulder.

Two hooks for thought and one to avoid and why

Shoulder choke

● This is the hook to drop. I know it's a favorite and you can still hit a green or tired player with it, so this is how to hit it correctly for argument's sake.Then we will run through a stalemate and a counter or two.

● You've done a double cross-face turnover and found your opponent's arm across his throat (here his left arm).

● Place your grapevines.

● Encircle his head with your left arm tightly.

● Use your chest to keep his arm pressed across his throat.

● Place the palm of your left hand onto your right biceps.

● Place your right hand behind your own neck, squeeze your elbows together, arch your back and stretch your grapevines to tap.

Shoulder choke stalemate

● As your opponent encircles your head with his left arm, simply insert a thumb (here your left) across your throat into his encircling biceps.

● This thumb hook creates a frame that will prevent his being able to finalize the choke (one thumb beats all that technique).

● Optional tactic — Groan and grimace to make him think that he is getting something accomplished and he will burn more energy. If you are lucky he will jump to the next move ...

Stacked shoulder choke

● Another move for you to avoid, but we will go through the motions so that you can easily counter this common attack.

● You are performing the shoulder choke from top saddle as before but can't seem to finalize.

● Leave your hands locked in place and hop your body from the mount to your right placing your left knee tight against his ribs and your right leg extended and posted for base at 90 degrees.

● Tighten your grip around his head and stack your weight through his throat to tap.

Two hooks for thought and one to avoid and why

Shoulder choke checkmate

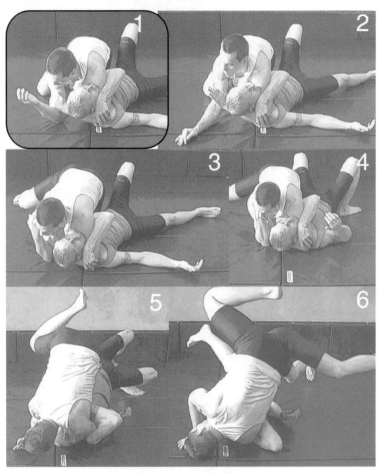

● You have inserted your thumb for the stalemate.
● Your opponent hops to the stacked shoulder choke position.
● Keeping your thumb inserted and taking advantage of his high hip base, bridge and roll at a 45 degree angle over your right shoulder.
● You are now in top position. Go to work.

68

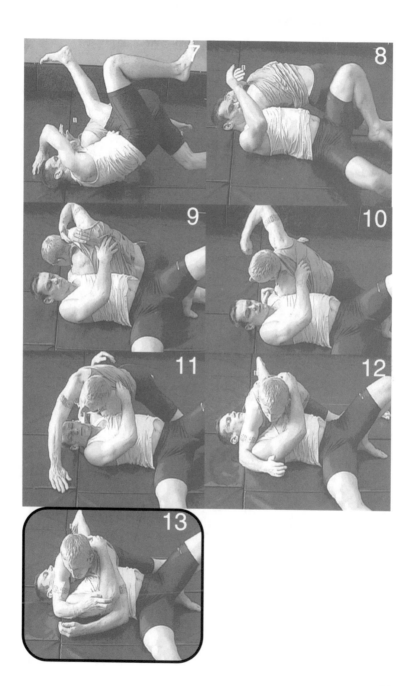

Two hooks for thought and one to avoid and why

Shoulder choke stalemate leg wrap

● When your opponent hops to the stacked shoulder choke, it is possible that your thumb will lose purchase.
● Rather than fight for reinsertion in what is now a tighter fit, pike your body and hug around your right knee with your free arm and clasp your hands.
● By keeping your knee hugged tightly you remove his choking leverage.
● To remove your arm from jeopardy, burst your hugged leg away at the same time you throw your trapped arm above your head.

4.5 Chain for Kazushi

The following chain is a tit for tat offensive/defensive series featuring one of the mainstays of Kazushi Sakuraba's arsenal. Trust me, we can all learn from this man. My hat is always off to him ... win, lose or draw.

Rear straight arm bar

● You are on your feet and he's on your back.

● Before he clasps his hands, grab one of them (here your right hand grabs his left).

● Keep his left arm overhooked above the elbow with the crook of your left arm.

● Figure-4 your hands, straighten your arms and arch your back into him while shooting your hips away to tap.

Rear straight arm beat

● I'm betting there are many folks in Pride history who wish they had this in their toolbox before playing Sak.

● Once caught in the rear straight arm bar (here your left arm is snagged) insert your right hand in the crook of his right arm and open your arm to the outside.

● This opening motion weakens the frame he needs for his submission.

● Don't merely use triceps strength to open. Lever your opening arm across his back to reduce your workload.

Rear straight arm offense/defense drill

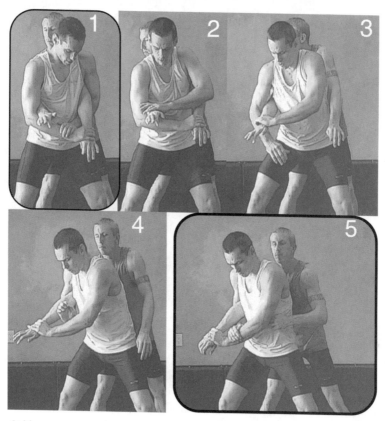

● Have your partner set a rear straight arm bar, you counter it, he shoots the arm bar on the counter arm, you re-counter and so on. Play it this way for a three-minute round and then switch positions.

When someone firsts hits the rear body lock, it's probably impossible to immediately snag a rear straight arm bar since their hands are locked. Following are a few ways to open the hands, but first and foremost, you must have your hips arched away from him throughout and your back driving into him hard. To do otherwise sets him up perfectly for *many* takedowns including the suplex (ouch!). Now on to opening the hands.

Resurrection

● Once he has locked his arms around you, in one concerted movement you must: thrust your hips away while shoving your upper back into him, arch your chest to the sky and throw your arms out to your sides to break his grip.
● Once his grip is broken, go for hand control.

Another view ...

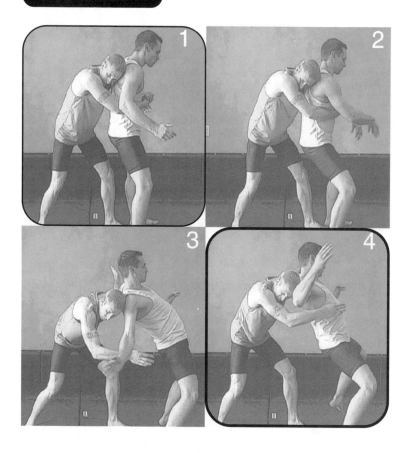

Three ways to gain hand control when you can't get resurrected

I won't cover the easily beaten bar grip here. You can find it in volume one.

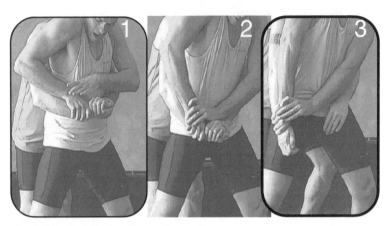

1. Attack his bottom hand

● Use both of your hands against his top control hand (here both of your hands versus his right).

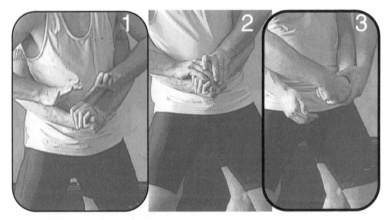

2. Attack his top hand

● Use both of your hands to attack his top hand.
● Insert your thumbs into his palm and roll his hand to the outside to gain hand control.

3. Forearm dig

● Your opponent has gripped higher on your chest making the fight for hand control tough.

● Work the points of your elbows into the tops of his forearms.

● Sink your weight through your elbows to open his grip and gain hand control.

Once you've gained hand control, you can shoot for the rear straight arm bar or use the shear turn to offer a new line of submissions.

Shear turn

● Once you've gained hand control (your left controlling his left in the following examples) raise your right arm high next to your head.

● Drop your hips and step your right foot behind your left.

● Swing with your right arm and turn toward your right to face him.

● Do not abandon your left wrist control while performing the turn.

● Once turned, drape your free right arm over his right shoulder — not over his arm.

Another view ...

● Important — Always turn away from your wrist control side into the arm that is still controlling your waist. By turning away from the seat belt arm you allow him to tighten its grip, and he can then suck you back into him for control or a takedown.

Shear turn to double wrist lock

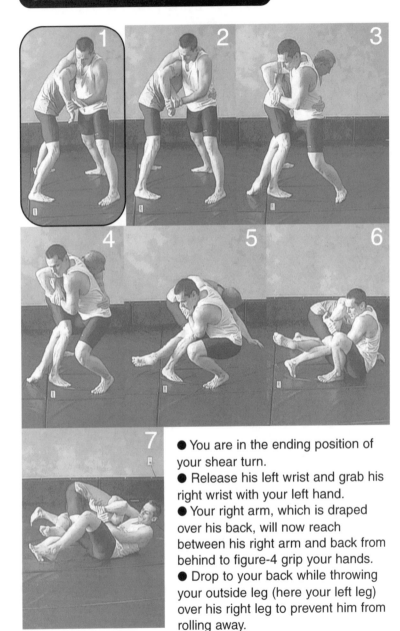

- You are in the ending position of your shear turn.
- Release his left wrist and grab his right wrist with your left hand.
- Your right arm, which is draped over his back, will now reach between his right arm and back from behind to figure-4 grip your hands.
- Drop to your back while throwing your outside leg (here your left leg) over his right leg to prevent him from rolling away.

● Arch your back and travel his arm in an outside arc toward his head to tap.

Shear turn to kick-over cross-body double wrist lock

● You have performed the first three movements of the preceding technique but have hit a snag. You are unable to overhook his right leg with your left, which will allow him to roll out of the hook.

● Keep your figure-4 set, and drop to the mat, kicking with your inside foot (here your right) toward the sky to elevate him over the top.

● Keeping your figure-4 grip, roll into a cross-body ride on his left side.

● Pull your elbows into his body, squeeze them together and twist his wrist to tap.

Another view ...

Chain for Kazushi

Shear turn to maximum crank

● You have completed your shear turn and have your right arm draped over his right shoulder, but you are concerned that he is circling toward your back.

● Bring your right arm from its draped position to encircle his head in the fashion of a guillotine choke.

● Pass his right arm toward your encircling right hand with your left by either:
1. Gripping his right wrist with your left and sending it across or
2. Wedging your left elbow on top of his right forearm and sending it across.

● Grip his passed right arm with your right hand at the triceps.

● Duck your head underneath his chest at his right side and (keeping your grip on his triceps and head) barrel roll over your left shoulder bringing your opponent down and over the top of you.

● Maintaining your grip on his head and arm and keeping your hips low, move to a cross-body ride on his left side.
● Pressuring him into a flat back position, look and arch over your right shoulder to tap.

Shear turn to cradle crunch

● You have completed your shear turn but have little hope of controlling his right arm.

● Bring your right arm from its draped position to encircle the head as in the previous technique.

● Turn the corner toward your opponent's right side, lower your base and overhook his right leg behind the knee with your left arm.

● As you attempt to clasp your hands in a standing near cradle, push into his ribs with your head to drop him to the mat. Important — Push with your head and not your upper chest. Pushing with your upper chest will cause you to hit the mat in an overbalanced position and he will be able to roll and reverse you.
● Once on the mat, secure your grip and keep a low cross-body to keep him pinned.

● Overhook his cradled leg (his right) with your left (overhook at the knee).
● Switch your grip to a T-grip (left hand grips right wrist).
● Turk his right leg with your left (arch it to the ceiling), straighten your arms, as if doing a diamond push-up, and arch your back to tap.

Wedge sag

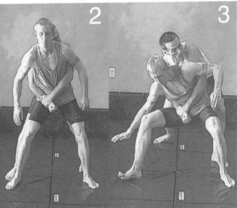

● To end this section I will provide an exceptionally easy drop to use when you attain the rear body lock position that most seem to bypass. It's the easiest and most effortless drop I know.

● Here you have the rear body lock position, are maintaining a base lower than your opponent's and keeping his hips sucked in tight to yours.

● Place the outer edge of your right forearm against the top of his thigh where it junctions with the hip.

● Build a frame with your arms by gripping your right wrist with your left hand.

● By applying downward pressure at this hip juncture you will drop your opponent almost effortlessly. Tip — Take him down at a 45 degree angle toward his right buttock.

4.6 Reverse cross-face series

Standard reverse cross-face

● You are on top and head to head with your opponent. Rather than hit a guillotine, under-hook his left shoulder with your right arm and overhook his right shoulder with your left.

● Turn the corner to your left (moving to his right side).

● Using the back of your underhooking right elbow, hit him on or above the ear line to crank his neck toward his right shoulder.

● With your elbow still wedging his head tight, overhook his right tri-ceps with your right hand.

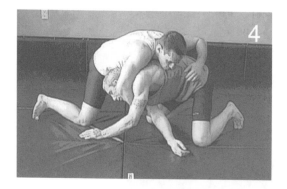

● Pull his right arm across his chest while you strive to take your right elbow back toward your right hip to tap. Important — Remember to keep your hips driving into him throughout.

Reverse cross-face free hand cinch #1

● Once you hit the end of the previous technique, it is some-times necessary to provide a little contrary motion to drive the pain home.

● Keeping all of the aforementioned movements in place, use your free left hand to grip the wrist of his trapped right arm.

● While performing the final step of the previous move, pull his right wrist toward the sky with your left hand to assist in the tap.

Reverse cross-face free hand cinch #2

● If you find the previous cinch troublesome, hit this one.
● Use your free left hand to underhook his left shoulder and grip the top of his deltoid mass (shoulder ball and socket joint).
● While performing the last movement of the first technique in this series, pull his left shoulder toward his left hip with your left hand to assist in the tap.

Reverse cross-face to top wrist lock

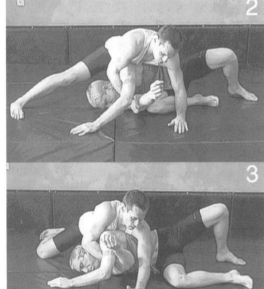

● You have arrived at the last position of the reverse cross-face hook. Your opponent is smart and realizes that the way out is to drop his right shoulder to the mat and attempt to roll toward you to take the pressure off his neck. (By the way, this can happen only if you are not applying enough pressure with your hips. Keep your hips snug and driving into him and there will be no roll. But always be prepared).

● As he dips his shoulder, drop your base. Apply pressure into him throughout. By doing this, you will keep him on his right side facing away from you rather than going to his back

forcing you to abandon this chain.

● Once he is on his side (make sure you maintain that hook on his right triceps the whole time) lift his right elbow with your right hand.

● Underhook his bent elbow with the crook of your left arm.

● Grab his right hand with your right hand (your thumb into his palm).

● Figure-4 grip your hands, drag your elbows into him, squeeze them together and twist his wrist to tap.

Missed top wrist lock to dorsal lock

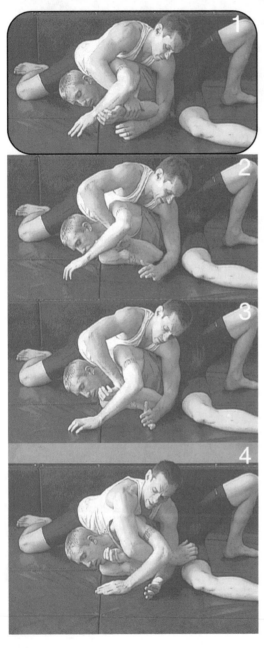

● Your opponent has dropped to escape the reverse cross-face, as in the previous move. You have either lost the hook on his triceps or cannot lift his arm to underhook his folded elbow.

● Underhook his folded left elbow with the crook of your left arm.

● Turn the corner around his head while keeping pressure on his body with your chest.

● Place your right knee on top of his pinned right hand and sit on his head.

Important — You must always pin the bottom arm to the mat with your knee before hitting any dorsal or dorsal variety lock. If you do not, he can easily come to base and resume the scramble.

● Grip his left hand with your left hand.

● Figure-4 grip your hands.

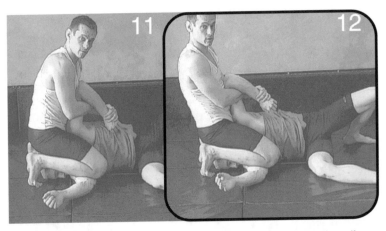

● Drag his arm straight back toward the top of his head until there is no more slack and then turn his left palm toward his back to tap. Important — You must always do this drag to the crown before turning to the back. Some players have a good deal of shoulder flexibility, but you will find that this slack remover increases the technique's efficiency.

Another view ...

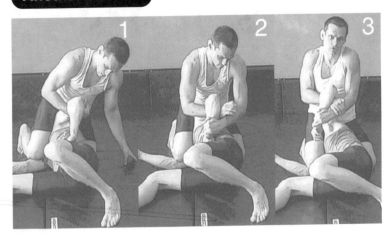

Dig to unblock a dorsal

● You're shooting the previous technique and your opponent is blocking you by grabbing his hands or grabbing his own trunks to prevent you from dragging his arm back (to remove the slack).

● Place the point of your back-side elbow (the elbow closest to his back, here the left) and dig it into his ribs.

● Once he releases his hands continue with the previous technique.

Dorsal head scissors

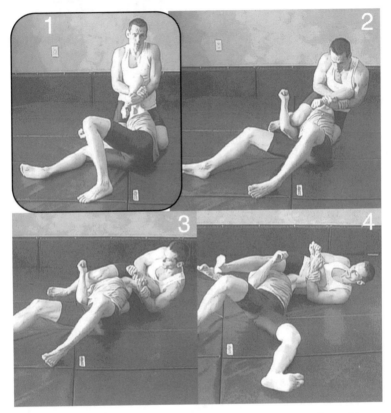

● While shooting for the dorsal your opponent may attempt to scramble to base.

● If during this scramble you feel your own base and balance compromised, maintain your figure-4 grip and fall toward his back onto your left side.

● Once you fall, straighten your legs while keeping his head scissored between your knees. Important — Make sure his head is not below or above your knees.

● Cross your feet at the ankle with your top foot crossed over your bottom foot (here your right over your left), straighten your legs hard, tighten the figure-4 grip on his arm and arch your hips to tap.

Another view ...

Dorsal head scissors to crocodile roll

● If your opponent does not tap on the final movement of the head scissors, maintain all your lockdown positions and log roll your body toward his hips thinking of going over his chest.

● By maintaining a tight head scissors and rolling toward his hips you will be lifting his head from the mat for an uncomfortable cervical kink that will result in a tap. Important — Hit the crocodile roll slowly. It hits hard and fast.

Dorsal to cross-body double wrist lock

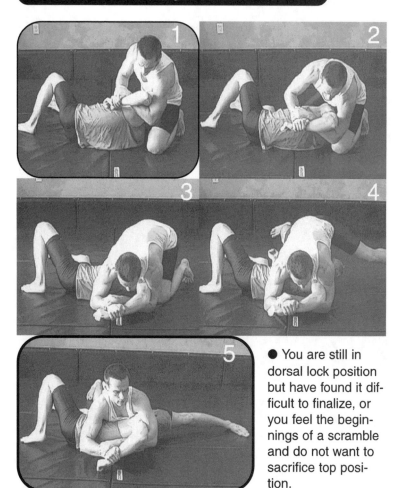

● You are still in dorsal lock position but have found it difficult to finalize, or you feel the beginnings of a scramble and do not want to sacrifice top position.

● Maintain your figure-4 grip on his arm and turn the corner toward his chest.
● As you turn you will flatten him out into a cross-body ride.
● While keeping your figure-4 grip, drag your elbows into his left side, squeeze them together and twist his hand to tap.

Dorsal to cross-body double wrist lock to SAS

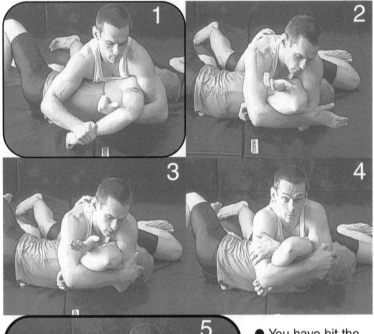

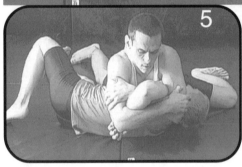

● You have hit the previous movement and have found the double wrist lock hard to finalize or your opponent is strong enough to decrease the angle in his arm.

● Shoot for the SAS by releasing your figure-4 grip and pointing the thumb of your left hand into the crook of his left elbow wedging your inner wrist tight into the crook of his arm.

● Overhook his left wrist with the crook of your right arm.

● Grip your triceps, squeeze your elbows together, while arching your chest through his arms to tap.

4.7 Reverse full nelson series

Reverse full nelson

● You are head to head with your opponent and you are in top position.

● Overhook each of his arms and drag your elbows toward his armpits causing his arms to travel away from his body.

● From this overhook position, place one hand and then the other on the back of his neck.

● Grip your hands behind his neck by grabbing your fingers in a barrel grip.

● Move your grip toward the back of his head. All nelsons should be levered on the back of the head rather than the back of the neck. This increases your leverage.

● Straighten your arms forcing his chin toward his chest and his arms above his head and push your hips through to tap.

Reverse full nelson with leg hook assist

● You have performed all the previous movements and find that you still cannot finalize.

● To increase your leverage, overhook one of his arms with one of your legs (here his right arm with your left leg) and use the added hook of your leg to turk that arm to tap.

Reverse full nelson into killing mount

● You have hooked your reverse full and have not been able to hit the tap.

● Keep your full nelson hook and drive into his head with your hips causing him to drop his hips back over his legs.

● Once he lands in a sitting position, keeping your hips low and your reverse full hook, continue to drive and step yourself into a quasi-mounted position. Your opponent will tap long before you settle into a low mount. Important — Work this move slowly. Take care of your training partners.

Reverse full nelson into cage mount

● This link in the chain is provided for those who train with cage walls or matted vertical surfaces.

● You perform the same drive through as in the previous move but here the opponent has resisted the drive over to his butt. Instead he continues to move backward to maintain base and run ahead of cervical kinking.

● Drive your opponent's rear end into the cage wall while keeping your reverse full hook.

● Once he is stacked securely into the wall, keep his head in the center of your abdomen and drive your hips through while straightening your arms to tap.

Reverse full nelson spreader

● This movement is provided for those occasions when you can only get one of your arms overhooked and into nelson position.
● Underhook his arm with your non-nelson arm (here your right arm underhooks his left arm).
● Turn your head toward your underhooking arm and place your left shoulder against the nape of your opponent's neck (and no lower).
● Sprawl to the mat and drive your shoulder through his neck while spreading his arms out and away from his body to tap.

4.8 Arm drag to floating sweep series

I advise performing all sweep motions off your back only after you have secured a solid arm drag position. Attempting gi-less sweeps with any other hand relationship often leads to slip-outs particularly once sweat starts pouring.

Securing an arm drag from the back

● Cross-reach for whichever of your opponent's arms is away from his torso. To cross-reach is to reach across your body for same limb versus same limb. In this case right versus right.

● Grip his triceps tight and drag his arm across your body (to your right) and at a 45 degree angle toward your right shoulder. Important — When performing an arm drag off your back, don't just pull with your arm and back muscles. Put your whole torso into the movement to increase the amount of drag power.

Floating sweep

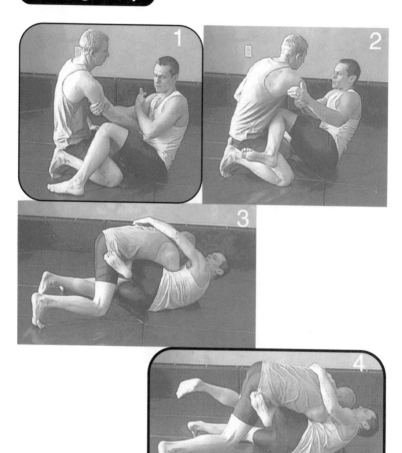

● You have already secured your arm drag and your opponent is tight to your body.

● Use your free hand (here your left) to reach across his back and grip his lat muscle on the left side of his back just below the arm pit.

● Open your legs and insert your left knee between your bodies. Your knee will be pointing toward your right and his weight will be resting on the outside of your inserted left thigh.

Arm drag to floating sweep series

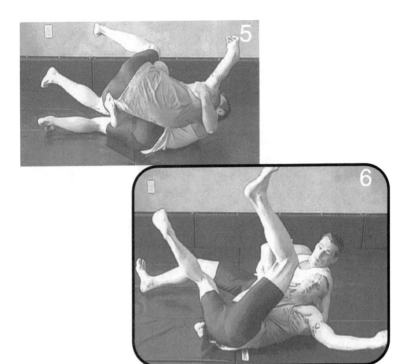

● Pull him by your lat grip to load him onto your left thigh.
● Once he is fully loaded, open your left leg hard toward your left side to sweep him to your left.
● Maintain your arm drag hook and cover him in a cross-body ride.

Floating sweep to top body/lateral press

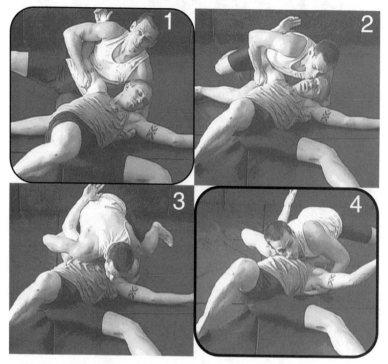

● Perform the first five moves from the previous technique.
● Once you sweep him, keep your arm drag and move to cover him in a top body/lateral press.

Floating sweep to top body/lateral press top wrist lock

● Once you hit the top body position, underhook his left arm that is still secured with your arm drag. Underhook with the crook of your right arm.

● Grab his left hand with your left hand being sure to place your thumb into the palm of his hand.

● Figure-4 your hands and sit-out onto your right hip taking his head out of line from his spine.

● Drag your elbows into him, squeeze them together and twist his hand toward you to tap.

Floating sweep to top body/lateral press head-to-head spreader

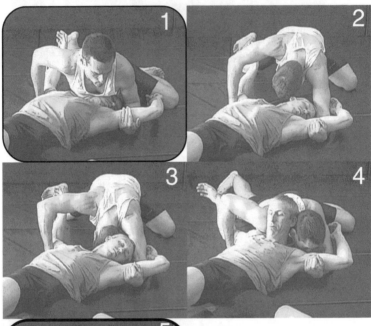

- Perform the floating sweep and maintain your arm drag.
- As you travel to the lateral press, stay low and slide your lat-gripping left hand up his back to underhook his left arm.
- Keeping his arms pulled above his head with your underhooking and overhooking grips, force your head underneath his head.
- Continue to pull his arms above his head and drive his chin toward his chest with your head to tap.

Floating sweep to far cross-body scoop

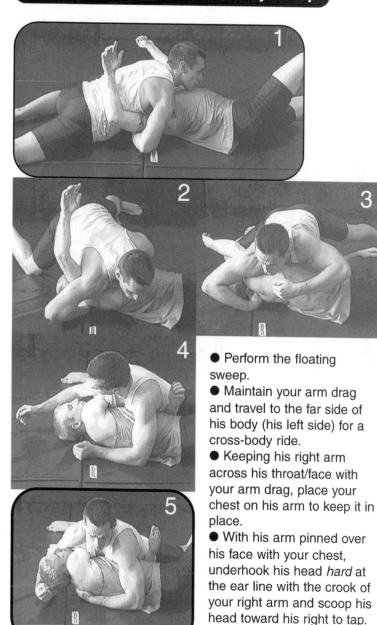

- Perform the floating sweep.
- Maintain your arm drag and travel to the far side of his body (his left side) for a cross-body ride.
- Keeping his right arm across his throat/face with your arm drag, place your chest on his arm to keep it in place.
- With his arm pinned over his face with your chest, underhook his head *hard* at the ear line with the crook of your right arm and scoop his head toward his right to tap.

Floating sweep to time hold with variations

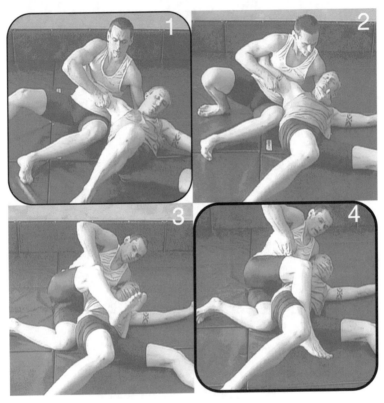

- Perform the floating sweep.
- As soon as your opponent is flat on his back, maintain your arm drag and hook his lat tighter with your left hand or ...
- Secure a chin hook with your left hand.
- Step your outside leg (here your right leg) between his legs to secure him from bridging or rolling away.
- Hug his bent elbow tight in the crook of your right arm and snug your right upper arm into your right side to increase the angle of bend in his arm.
- Pull your lat or chin hook tight, cinch his arm and bridge your hips to the sky to tap.

Time hold anti-bridging variation

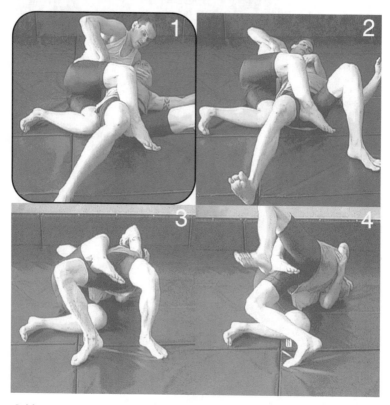

● You are performing the previous movement and your opponent attempts to bridge-step over you to escape the tap.
● During his bridge-step, use your stepped right foot as an elevator and kick to the sky to place him on his back again.
● Cinch your grips and tap as in the previous move.

Arm drag to floating sweep series

Time hold near-leg secure variation #1

● The following variations of the time hold differ only in the ways you use your securing leg. In both, the near leg is used and may lead to your opponent having an easier time escaping with a bridge-step.

● In this variation, the near leg (here your left) steps between your opponent's legs.
● Follow the usual grip steps to tap.

Time hold near-leg secure variation #2

● Here, your near leg steps across your opponent's abdomen.

Arm bar versus blocked floating sweep

● You have set up your floating sweep and as you rock back to hit it, your opponent begins running toward your open side (away from the inserted knee — here to your right).

● Maintain your arm drag and release your lat grip with your left hand.

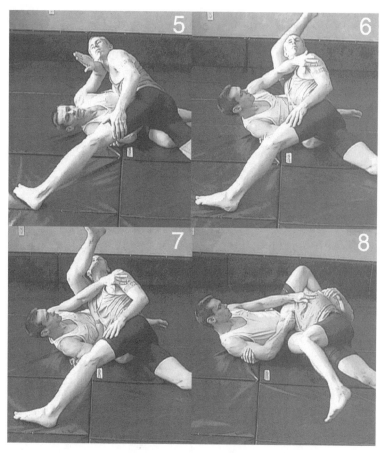

● Using the outside of your forearm, shove his face toward your right and frame it there with your left forearm.

● Rock your weight onto your right shoulder and swing the back of your left leg over in front of his face to take the place of your left forearm.

● Keeping his chin tight in the back of your left knee, kick your left leg toward the mat bringing him to his back.

Arm drag to floating sweep series

● Keep a tight arm drag grip, his head flat to the mat with your left leg, point your right knee toward the sky while keeping your shin wedged into his ribs, squeeze your knees together and arch your hips to tap.

Head-to-head roll versus aggressive passed floating sweep

● Your opponent has passed quickly toward your open side and moved beyond the point where you can set up the straight arm bar.

● As he approaches top body/lateral press position, keep your arm drag tight while attempting to secure his left arm by overhooking it with your left.

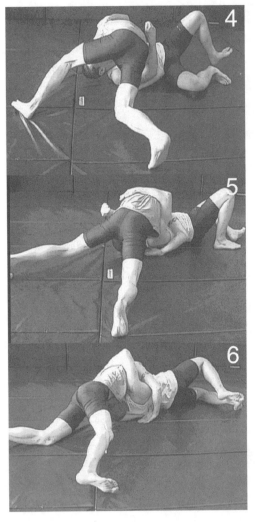

● Use the inertia of his movement to top position to barrel roll him to your left bringing you to top body control. From there you can ride or hit movements 2, 3, or 4 of this series.
● You can also use the turn the corner series from here.

4.9 Squatting series

Set up from top saddle

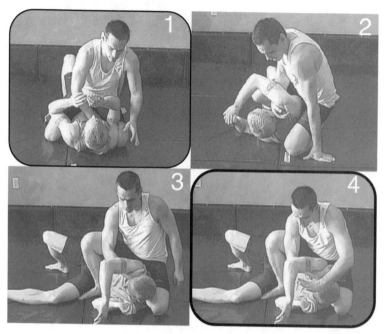

● You are in top saddle/mounted position on your opponent and he attempts to barrel roll to either side (here to his left).

● Open your right leg scissors slightly to allow him to get as far as his left side.

● Immediately shift your weight by sliding your left knee even with the crown of his head and sitting on your left haunch staying tight to your opponent.

● You also point your right knee toward the sky and post your right foot on the mat dragging it tight into his abs. Important — Stay tight to him with this foot. Leave *no* space.

● Stay low throughout to keep your base.

● While performing the above place your right hand on the front of your opponent's right deltoid. As he turns to his left, his right arm will be underhooked by your right arm.

Hanging wrist lock

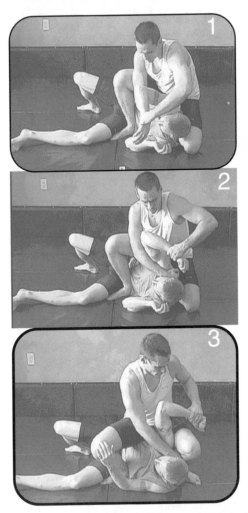

● Grab his right hand with your left hand.

● Step either your right foot or right knee on top of his left arm to prevent his rolling. Rise to a squatting position seating your weight on top of his ribs.

● Lever his right hand toward his back while pointing your left knee to his chest through his right shoulder to tap.

Mighty head crank

- Reach behind his head with your left hand and grip his right wrist.
- Maintain a tight grip on his right hand with your left and reach around his head with your right hand dragging your right inner forearm blade across his face.
- Reach as deep as you can around his head with your right and grip your left forearm with your right hand (use a thumbless grip to allow for greater rotation in this technique).
- Maintain your grips and straighten your arms. The pinching action of your arms, in effect, forces a cross-face variant tap.

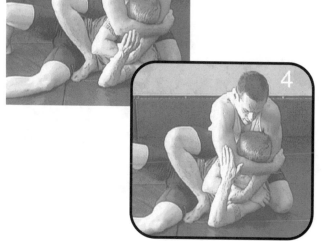

Figure-4 legs short arm scissors (SAS)

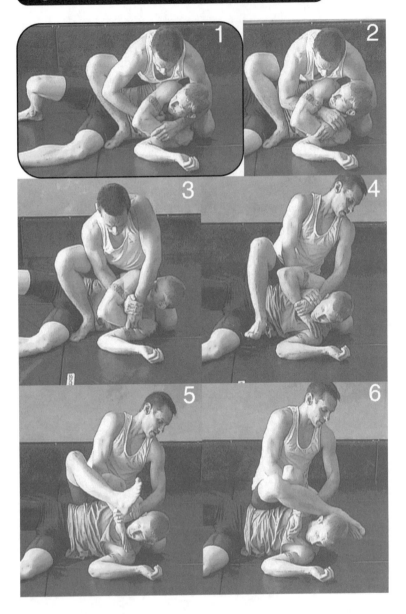

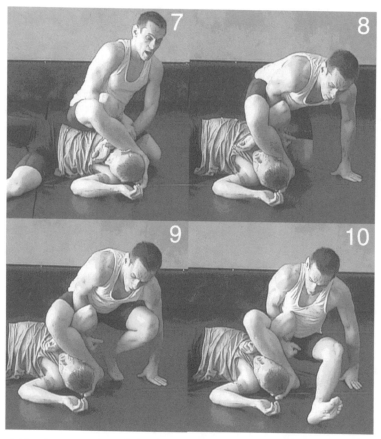

● You have moved to the set up position from the top saddle.
● Grab his right wrist with your left hand and figure-4 your hands.
● Stay with me here, this is an odd one, but it hits hard. Keeping his captured arm low, step your right foot behind his head being sure to keep his captured right forearm wedged tightly behind your right calf.

● You will fall to your back while figure-4ing your right ankle behind your left knee.

● Switching your hands from a figure-4 grip, leave your right wrist wedged in the crook of his right arm and apply a palm-to-palm grip.

● Squeeze your knees together and pull your wedged right forearm through his elbow to tap.

Falling arm bar

● Here is a standard arm bar, but it is shown last in the series because I strongly advise you not make any technique where you remove weight from your opponent a first choice. Cross arm bars are fine but strive to be a player that can hit hooks from top dominant positions so you have run-to moves like the arm bar.
● Hit the set up from the top saddle.
● Place your left palm on your opponent's face forcing him to look away from you (here to his left).

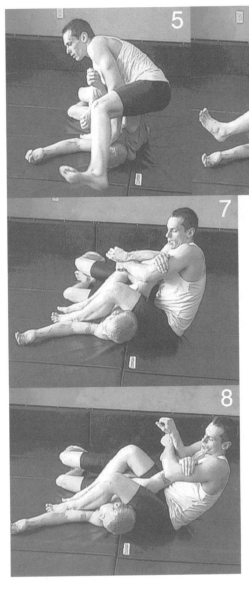

● Place all your weight through his head with your left hand and swing your left leg in a low smooth arc around and across his face. Important — If you have placed yourself in strict set-up position, the arc will be smooth and without the herky-jerky of arm bars that appear to be more of a step-over than a swing-over. Step-overs allow for a momentary lapse of pressure on your opponent allowing him escape opportunities, whereas the swing-over maintains pressure all the way.

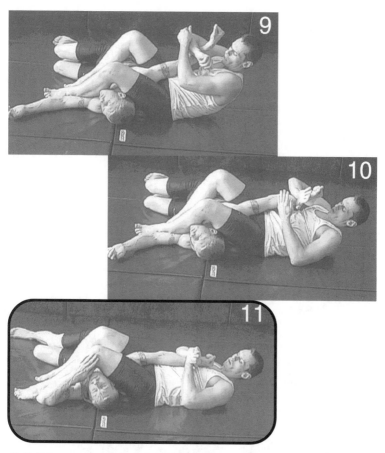

● Fall to your back being sure to keep your hips as tight to his shoulder as you can manage.

● Place your feet on either side of his far arm in a splayed kick-stand position to provide stability for his potential bridging.

● Squeeze your knees together and slide your right inner wrist up to his right inner wrist.

● Apply a palm-to-palm grip and dig in hard against his wrist (this removes the onus of having to make sure that his hand is in a thumbs up/little finger down relationship).

● Dig his hand into your chest, squeeze your knees together and arch your hips to tap.

4.10 Arm bar helpers

Optimally you will hit an arm bar as the last movement in a submission chain since it forces you to
remove weight from your opponent. When you do
hit an arm bar, aim to be scrupulous with your technique as in the preceding move. There are times
though when your opponent is able to resist by
clasping his hands together to prevent you from hitting the full arm bar. The following chain runs
through several ideas on how to rectify and tap that
problem.

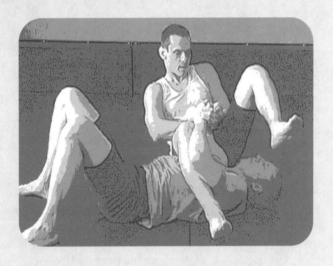

Kick stand

● Place your head-side foot (here your left foot) on his face or place your heel directly into his right jugular and shove.

Biceps kick

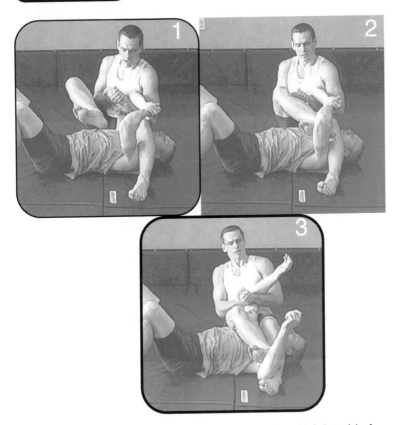

● Use your hip-side foot (here your right foot) to kick into his far biceps (his left biceps) to break his grip. Remember it is a kick not a shove.

Hammer the face

● Retain his arm with your hip-side arm (here your right arm) and use your left hammer fist to strike his face.

Hammer the groin

Heel drop to face

● Use the hip-side hammer fist to hammer your opponent's groin.

● Hit a heel drop to your opponent's face with your head-side heel.

Heel drop to solar plexus

● Hit a heel drop with your hip-side leg to his solar plexus.

Slap 'n pop

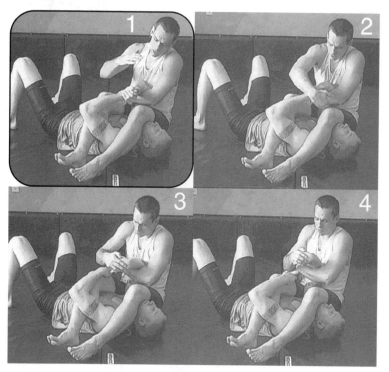

● Attack your opponent's nearest wrist.

● Retain his near-side arm with either your right or left under-hook (here your left underhook).

● It helps if he is stalemating by gripping his own wrists but it will work with other grips as well. Slap down and into his knuckles with your right hand. Think slapping toward his chest and then circling toward your own chest.

● When his grip releases, keep his knuckles firmly planted in the palm of your right hand and keep the back of his right elbow rooted tightly into the center of your chest.

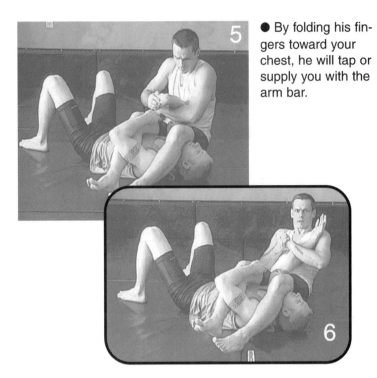

● By folding his fingers toward your chest, he will tap or supply you with the arm bar.

Top wrist travel

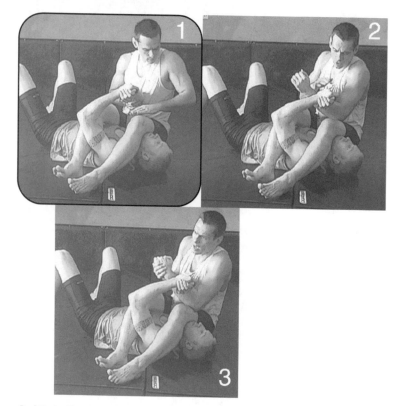

● Attain the arm bar by utilizing the principle that your opponent cannot be strong in two angles at once.

● Underhook his near-side wrist (his right) with your head-side wrist (your left) and place the inner cutting bone of your wrist against his inner cutting bone.

● Clasp your hands in a palm-to-palm grip.

● Lean toward the crown of his head with your entire body weight tugging on his arm. Next sweep in an out-ward arc around and then toward your back to break his grip. Hit the full arm bar.

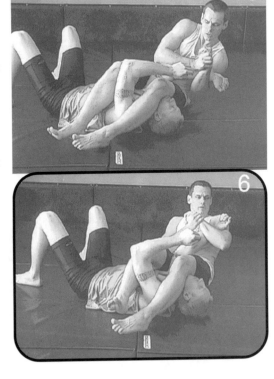

Pencil neck assistance

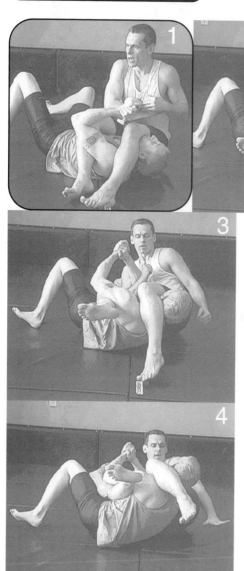

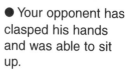

● Your opponent has clasped his hands and was able to sit up.

● Secure his arm with your hip-side underhook (here your right).

● Reach behind his neck with your left hand and grab your ankle, not your foot (too much give). Either cinch pressure to choke or pull him back to the mat and hit any of the arm bar helpers.

Arm bar helpers

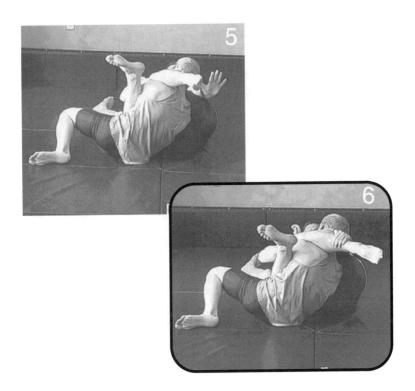

Leg popper

● Your opponent has managed to sit up as in the previous technique.

● Rather than keep a single underhook on his arm, keep both arms underhooked.

● To send him back to the mat ballistically, straighten your head-side leg (your left). The impact of your hamstring will drop him back to the mat for you to finish your arm bar.

● Important — You are not swinging your leg back into him but straightening it hard to drop him.

Arm bar helpers

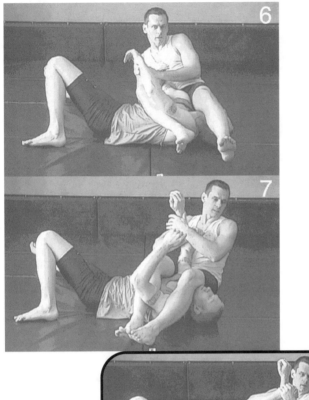

Figure-4 legs short arm scissors and a warning

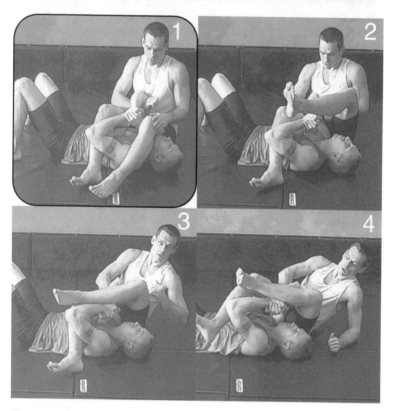

There are two ways to hit a figure-4 legs short arm scissors. The right way and the wrong way. The preferred technique is shown first and then the less effective version, followed by the simple counter to the second version that makes it a scrapped move.

● Your opponent has gripped his arms to stalemate your arm bar.

● Keep his arms underhooked with your arms but strive to place the inner cutting bone of your wrist (here your right wrist) deeply into the crook of his attacked arm.

● Place the back of your head-side calf (your left calf) on top of his folded right forearm.

Arm bar helpers

● Place the ankle of your left foot behind your hip-side knee (right knee). Important — Place the ankle *not* the foot behind your right knee. It's a harder lever and your foot won't be sacrificed in a scramble.

● Place the instep of your right foot underneath his right side just above his hip bone. This foot placement assists in preventing him turning into you.

● Tighten your figure-4 using your legs to force his right wrist toward his right biceps. Levering his folded arm over your inserted right wrist will set the tap.

Another view ...

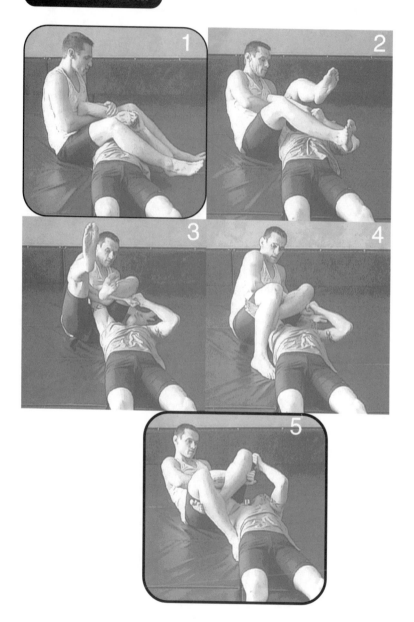

A figure-4 legs SAS to avoid

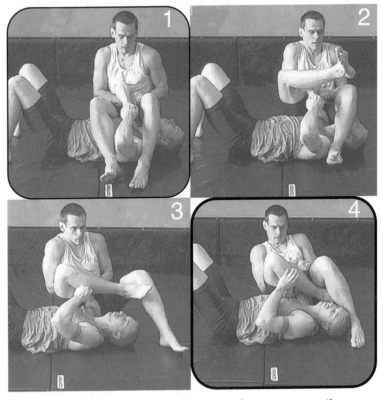

● Swing your hip-side leg over the top of your opponent's folded right arm.

● You figure-4 your right ankle behind your left knee, tighten your figure-4 and pull your wrist lever through his arm to tap.

Figure-4 SAS release

● This counter only works against the second version of the figure-4 SAS. The first provides too much stability to utilize the tip.

● Once the opponent has set his figure-4 SAS, momentarily release your stalemate grip and post your far hand (here your left hand) on the outside of his crossed-over knee (the knee on top of your arm — in this case, the right knee).

● With your left hand shove his knee hard at a 45 degree angle over your head as you bridge in the same direction and turn into him to attain a cross-body ride.

Arm bar with near foot included

● This and the next technique assume that your opponent is utilizing a stalemate grip and has both of his feet on the mat to hit a bridge in an attempt to shrug you off (not the best choice).

In both of these techniques you will have your head-side arm (your left arm) overhooking his attacked arm.
● Keeping your left arm overhook tight, lunge with your body to overhook his near ankle (his right).

Keep his ankle with the inner cutting forearm bone of your inner wrist, not in the crook of your arm.

● By lunging your body back to a line perpendicular to his shoulders and dragging his caught ankle with you, you will either provide enough uncomfortable torque on his near-side knee and hip that the arm bar can be completed; or you can keep both of your overhooks and grip your hands in a palm-to-palm grip (your ankle overhook palm will be on top facing toward the mat).

● Crank your inner cutting bone toward your heart to tap or facilitate the arm bar.

Arm bar helpers

Arm bar with far foot included

● You have lunged for his near foot and he removes this post.
● Continue to reach under his near leg (his right) and overhook his far leg (his left).
● Use the same inner cutting bone principles in your overhook.
● Drag his leg back to the perpendicular and follow the last two steps of the previous technique.

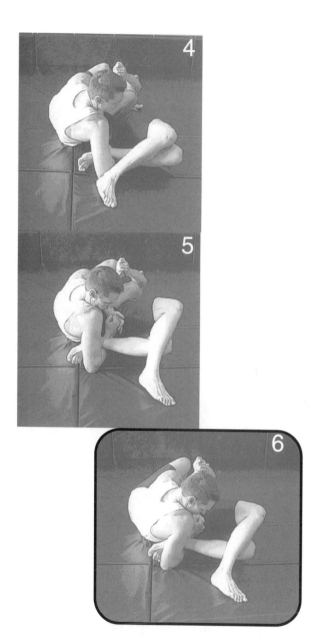

4.11 Hanging leg lock series

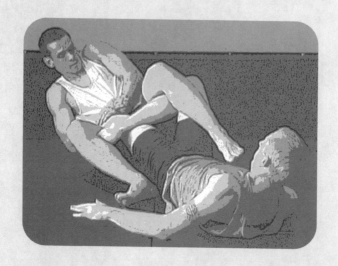

Hanging leg lock

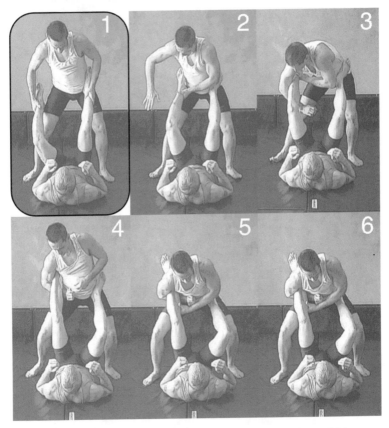

● You are inside your opponent's bottom scissors/guard. You are on your feet or on your knees and have snagged a foot and then go to your feet. Snagging means that you have one of his legs overhooked at the ankle. Here his left leg is overhooked.

● *Do not* fall back for a standard ankle/foot lock. This class of submission is easy to beat.

● Instead, keep his left foot trapped tight to your right side with inward pressure from your right upper arm. Do not simply lift on his foot "guillotine" style to keep him there.

● Step close to his hips with your right foot and post your left hand on his right knee.

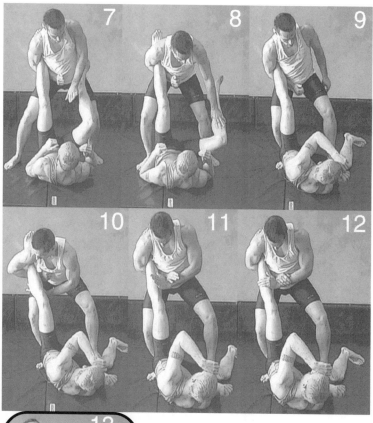

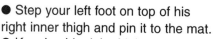

● Step your left foot on top of his right inner thigh and pin it to the mat.
● Keeping his right thigh pressured to the mat with your left foot, figure-4 grip your hands (being sure to point the inner cutting blade of your right forearm toward the sky into the back of his calf). Cinch your grip and arch your back as you look skyward to tap.

Front figure-4 knee bar toe hold

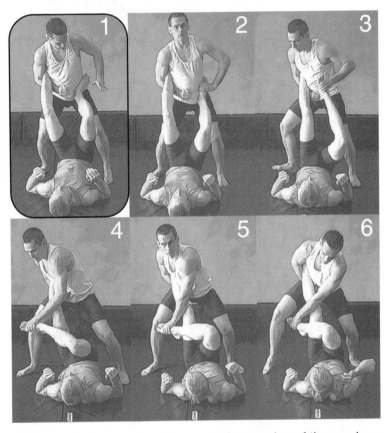

● You are in the same position as in the opening of the previous technique. But now your opponent is playing a smarter game and posts his free right foot on your left hip. He can keep a surprising amount of control by doing this.

● Maintain your overhook on his left foot with your right arm and grab the toes of his right foot with your left hand.

● Advance his right foot across and in front of his left knee by dragging his foot with your toe grip. Step your left foot toward his hips and advance your left hip toward his left knee to facilitate the movement.

● Once the foot is in place, overhook the toes of his right foot with the back of your right knee by stepping your right foot forward.

● Release his toes with your left hand and use that hand to grab the inside of his right knee and pull it toward you.

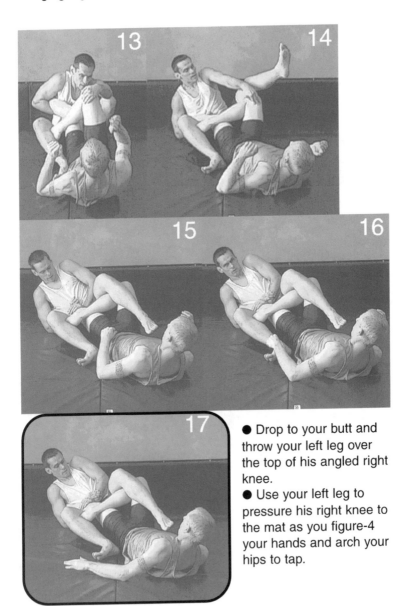

● Drop to your butt and throw your left leg over the top of his angled right knee.

● Use your left leg to pressure his right knee to the mat as you figure-4 your hands and arch your hips to tap.

Step-over crank

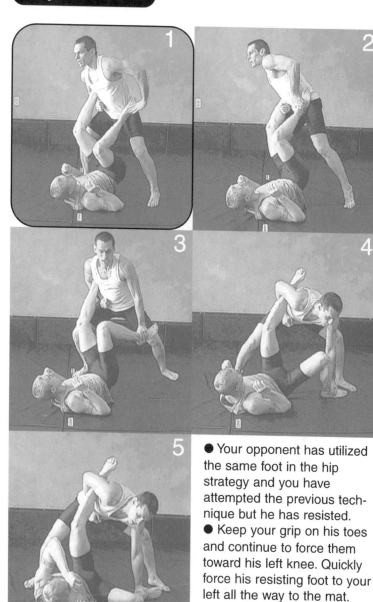

● Your opponent has utilized the same foot in the hip strategy and you have attempted the previous technique but he has resisted.

● Keep your grip on his toes and continue to force them toward his left knee. Quickly force his resisting foot to your left all the way to the mat. (Not that hard since he is defending the other direction).

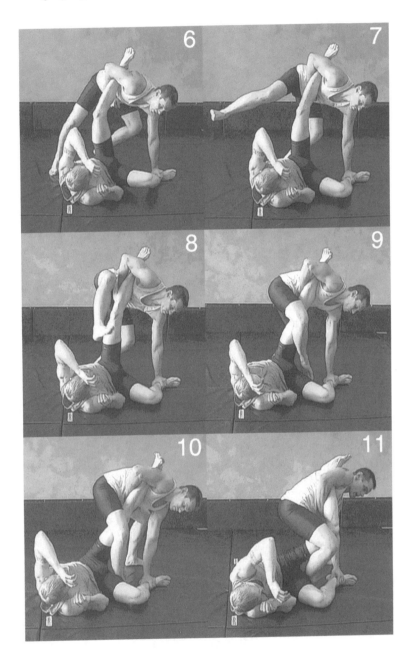

● Post your left hand on top of his right foot pinning it to the mat.

● Step your right leg over his still overhooked left leg.

● Wedge the toes of your right foot underneath the thigh of his pinned right leg.

● Place your left hand on the front of his left knee, sit back toward his lumbar spine, point your right knee toward your left and lift up on his knee to tap.

4.12 Back to basics

There are many ways to finish an opponent once you have gained his back. Many of these finishes have to do with hooks-in rides. Here we provide a chain for a non-hooked back ride working from the cockle-burr.

Cockle-burr

● The cockle-burr is not a submission but a ride used when your opponent has prevented the insertion of your hooks or when you choose to forego hooks.

● Back mount your opponent and arch your hips through.

● Run your insteps along the inside of his legs in a grapevine variant in which your toes are overhooked about six inches below his knees and your knees are on the outside of his legs pinching tight.

● If he tries to come to all fours, you have the options of inserting hooks, surfing to a cross-body ride or merely spreading out his legs with your insteps in this cockle-burr ride.

Sleeper

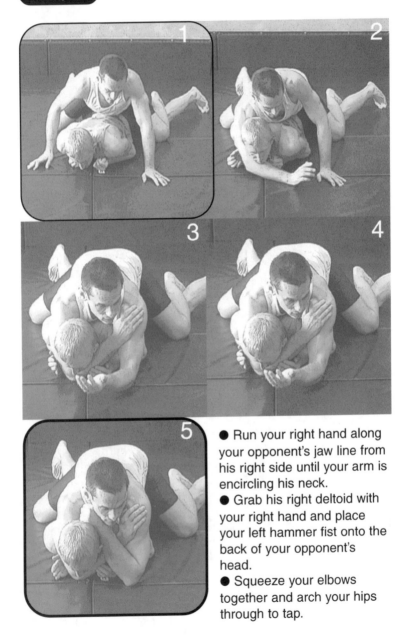

● Run your right hand along your opponent's jaw line from his right side until your arm is encircling his neck.

● Grab his right deltoid with your right hand and place your left hammer fist onto the back of your opponent's head.

● Squeeze your elbows together and arch your hips through to tap.

One-on-one choke

● Here you will control one of your opponent's wrists to prevent his defending the choke or coming to base as easily as he might with both hands free.

● Place the point of your elbow into the meaty tissue between your opponent's shoulder blades. This will cause his chin to raise and loosen his arms next to his body.

● Keeping the dig in place, underhook his left arm with your left and grab his left wrist with your left.

● Underhook his throat with your right arm.

● Grab your left deltoid mass with your right hand, tighten your grip around his throat and arch your hips through to tap.

Turn the corner cutter

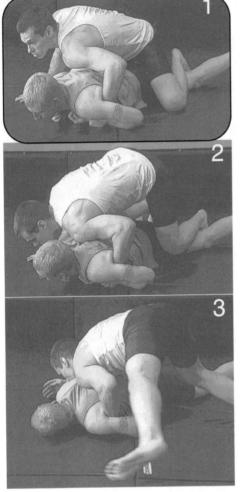

● You have the one-on-one but have been unsuccessful in the one-arm choke.

● Maintain the one-on-one with your left hand.

● Place the point of your left shoulder directly between his shoulder blades and post *all* of your weight through that shoulder.

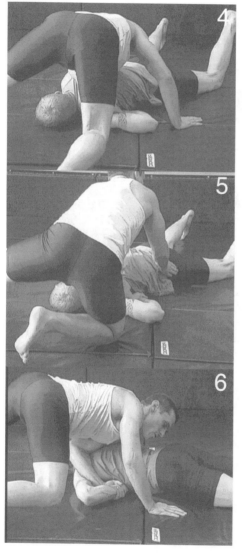

● Using your left shoulder as a pivot point, raise your hips and turn the corner to your left and toward the top of his head. Important — Do not go to your knees or take your weight off your pivot point at any time during this transition.
● Assist your left hand one-on-one grip by grabbing your left hand with your right.

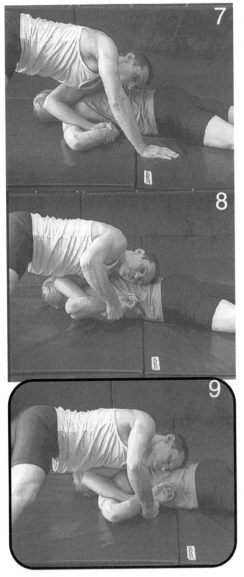

- Pull his left arm out from his body at a 90 degree angle with his arm pointing toward his hips (his palm will be facing up).
- Without releasing your grip on his hand, place the outer cutting bone of your left forearm perpendicular across his upper left arm. Important — It must be perpendicular and not at an angle as that mitigates the cutting pressure of your forearm. It will be uncomfortable but not necessarily tapable.
- Shift your weight from your left shoulder pivot point to your left cutting bone once it is in position. As your drive all of your weight through his left upper arm with your cutting bone, lift his left palm skyward to tap.

Thigh cram

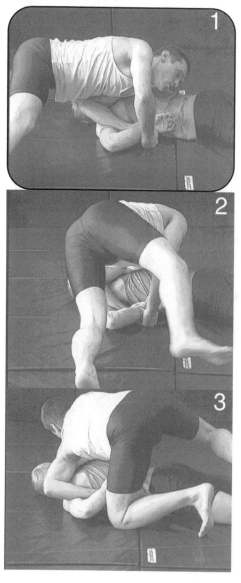

● You have shot for the cutter but find that your opponent is keeping his left arm tight to his body. This disallows good forearm placement for the cutter.

● Post your left shoulder pivot point and turn the corner again toward his back attempting to lift his left elbow from the mat as you go.

● Once you have turned the corner, sit on his back and jam your left knee under his lifted left elbow.

● With your left knee under his elbow, use both of your hands to lift his left hand from under his body and on to his back.

● From here we have three options:

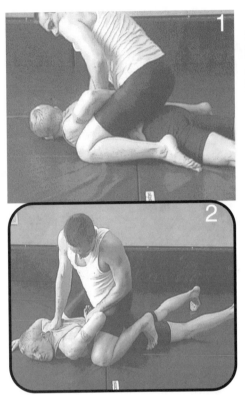

1. Lifted hammer

● Keep your left knee tight under his left elbow and lift his left hand skyward to tap.

2. Knee pressure hammer

● Once his left hand is on his back, keep it gripped and place your left knee on top of his left elbow.

● Lift his left hand toward the sky while putting downward pressure on his elbow with your left knee to tap.

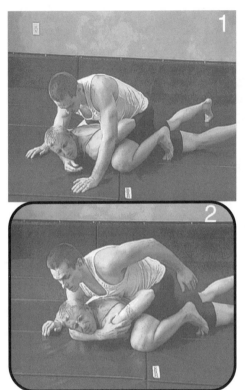

3. Cram and cross-face

● Leave your left knee under his left elbow.

● Underhook his face with the inner cutting bone of your right forearm forcing his face to look left.

● Force this cross-face deeper while jamming your knee tighter under his arm and driving your hips up his back to tap.

Maximum turnover crank

● You have again turned the corner and have set your thigh cram, but meet with a lot of scramble resistance that makes some of the previous thigh cram finishers seem iffy.

● Drive his left hand up his back and then post on top of his left hand with both of your hands.

● Put all of your weight through your hands and pop up to a diamond push-up position.

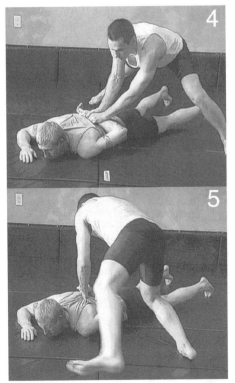

● Turn the corner to your left toward the top of his head.

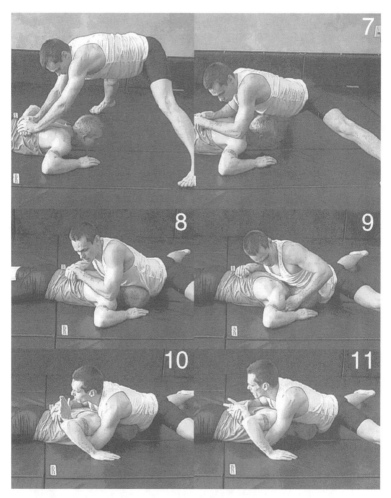

● When you reach the top of his head, retain his left hand with your right hand and drop to a face-down, lateral-press/top body hold.

● Maintain your grip on his left hand and underhook his right shoulder with your left arm.

● Tip — If he is keeping his right arm tight to his side preventing your underhook, use the inside of your left elbow to shove his head toward your right. This will allow you to sneak in your underhook.

● Run your left under-hook as deep as you can get it and then grip his left hand with your left hand.

● Release his left hand with your right hand and overhook his head from your right side. Hook deep and tight.

● Maintain your head and hand grips and turn the corner toward your left. Get perpendicular to his shoulders and use chest pressure through him to roll him onto his back.

● Cinch your grips and arch your back looking over your head-side shoulder (here your right shoulder) to tap.

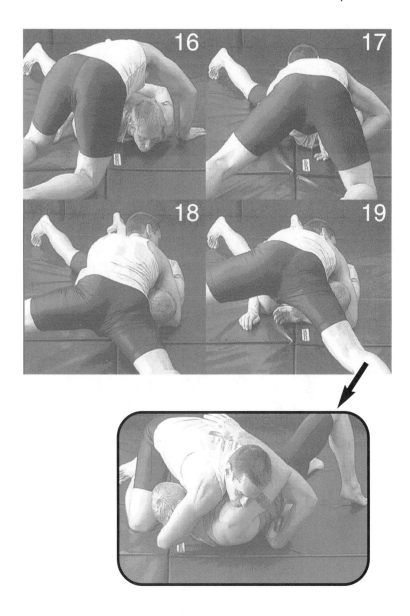

4.13 Lullaby chain

The following short chain is used to educate proper form in the various ways of attacking with a rear naked choke. I suggest working it in an A-B-C manner with one move following the other aiming for speed. Work it right and left sides.

Rear naked choke

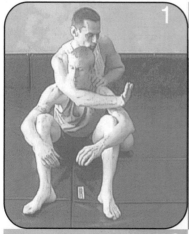

This technique is not actually part of the lullaby chain, but is shown to illustrate the differences between the standard rear naked choke and the sleeper choke. The rear naked choke works and is not ready for the scrap heap by any stretch of the imagination. It's just that the sleeper works more efficiently and with so much less effort that it should be your go-to choke from the back.

● Encircle your opponent's throat with the crook of your right arm, being sure to place the **V** of the throat (the hyoid bone) in the **V** of the crook of your right arm.

● Bring your left arm over your opponent's left shoulder and place the palm of your right arm onto the biceps of your left arm.

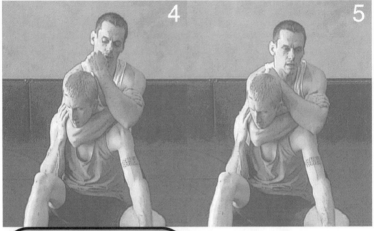

● Place the palm of your left hand on the back of your opponent's head.
● Squeeze your elbows together and arch your chest through your opponent as if doing a seated row to tap.

Sleeper

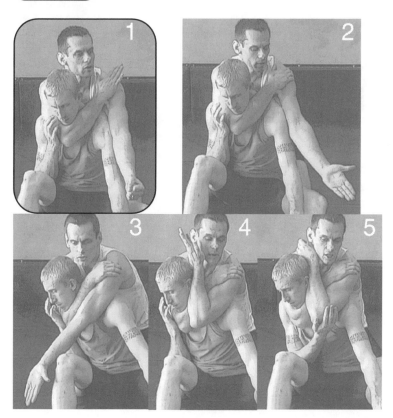

● Encircle your opponent's throat with the crook of your right arm being sure to place the **V** of his neck tight into the crook of your arm.

● Drape your left arm over his left shoulder and with your right hand grip the deltoid mass of your left shoulder (*not* your left biceps). Snug your grip around his throat.

● Sweep your extended left arm palm up across his chest toward your right. Think of striking the left side of your opponent's neck with the inside of your left elbow.

● Leaving your arm in the palm up position and tight to his neck with the extra inches gained by the sweeping motion, bend your left elbow and place your left hammer fist on the back of your opponent's head.

Lullaby chain

● Squeeze your elbows together, force your left hammer fist through the back of his head and crunch forward with your abs to tap.

Reverse lever choke

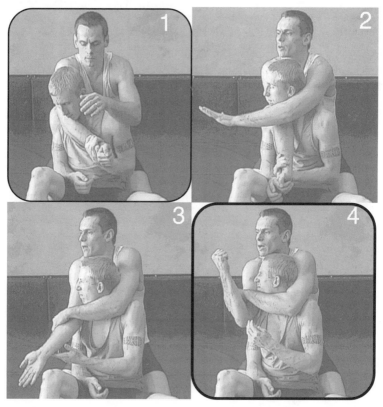

● Your opponent has inserted a hand between his throat and your right arm or is pulling on your right arm to alleviate some pressure.

● Bring your left hammer fist from behind his head.

● Sweep your right arm palm up toward the right side of his neck.

● With your left hand palm down, grip the top portion of your inner forearm.

● Perform a biceps curl with your right arm and arch your chest through him to tap.

● Tip — Your left arm does not have to be under his jaw to tap with the reverse lever.

Cross-face crank

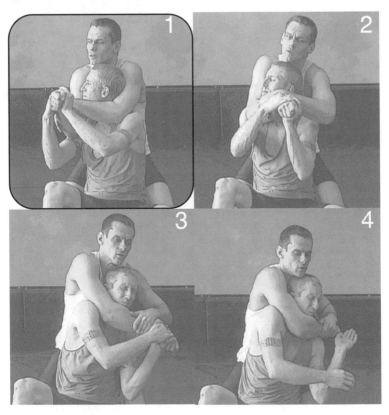

● Your opponent is levering down on your right arm to prevent the reverse lever.

● Sweep your right arm across his face driving the inner blade of your forearm across his face. The specific path of your forearm consists of sliding your forearm across his face, entering at the jaw on his right side and traveling diagonally upward across his nose to make him face left.

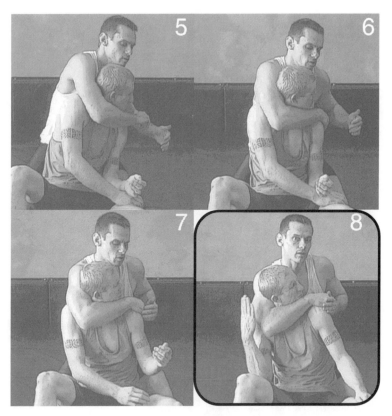

● Grip his left deltoid mass with your right hand.
● Continue to lever his face to the left while arching your chest through to tap.

Jaw cutter

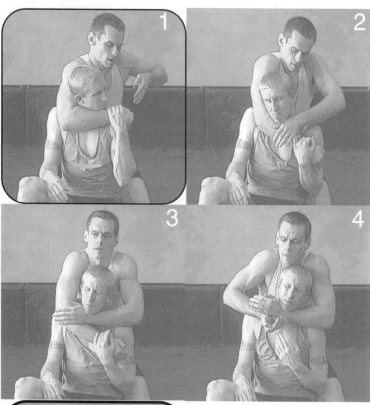

● Your cross-face crank has met with little success.
● Place the inner cutting bone of your left wrist underneath your opponent's jaw.
● Grip your left hand with your right in a palm-to-palm grip.
● Brace the back of his head against your upper chest by hunching your chest forward.
● Pull your left inner wrist upward (not inward) through his jaw to tap.

Reverse cross-face

● Leverage isn't right for the jaw cutter.
● Bring your right arm behind his head and encircle his face from his left side with the back of your upper right arm.

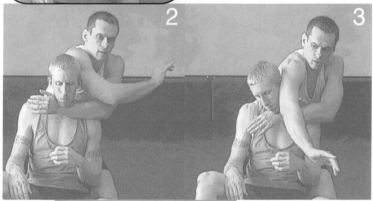

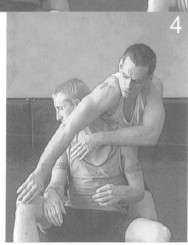

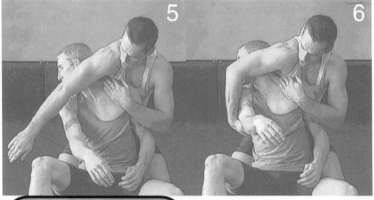

● Grip his right upper arm with your right hand.
● Arch your chest through him, pull his right arm with your right and seek to drive your right elbow toward your right side to tap.

NHB / submission wrestling resources

BEST CHOICES

First, please visit my Web site at **www.extremeselfprotection.com** You will find even more training material as well as updates and further resources. Let me know if you have any questions, comments or concerns about the material in this book or about any topic regarding training.

Amazon.com
The place to browse for books such as this one and other similar titles.

Tony Cecchine
www.catchwrestle.com
Another quality resource.

Paladin Press
www.paladin-press.com
Paladin carries many training resources. They carry some of my videos which will allow you to see much of what is covered in my NHB books.

Ringside Boxing
www.ringside.com
Best choice for primo equipment.

Sherdog.com
Best resource for MMA news, event results and current NHB happenings.

Threat Response Solutions
www.trsdirect.com
Same as above. They offer many training resources, among them some of my products.

Tracks Publishing
www.startupsports.com
Tracks publishes this book and its prequel and has other fine books including a couple of boxing titles.

www.humankinetics.com
Training and conditioning information.

www.matsmatsmats.com
Best resource for quality mats at good prices.

GENERAL

Equipment

Everlast
718-993-0100

Fairtex
www.fairtex.com

Ringside
1-877-4-BOXING
www.ringside.com

Magazines

Fight Sport
fightsportmag.com

Full Contact Fighter
fcfighter.com

Grappling

Books

Boxer's Start-Up:
A Beginner's Guide to Boxing
by Doug Werner

Brazilian Jiu-Jitsu:
The Master Text
by Gene "Aranha" Simco

The Fighter's Notebook
by Kirik Jenness and David Roy

No Holds Barred: Evolution
by Clyde Gentry III

No Holds Barred Fighting:
The Ultimate Guide to
Submission Wrestling
by Mark Hatmaker

Video instruction

Extreme Self-Protection
extremeselfprotection.com

Paladin Press
paladin-press.com

Panther Productions
panthervideos.com

Threat Response Solutions
trsdirect.com

World Martial Arts
groundfighter.com

Events

IFC
ifc-usa.com

IVC
valetudo.com

King of the Cage
kingofthecage.com

Pancrase
so-net.ne.jp/pancrase

Pride
pridefc.com

The Ultimate Fighting
Championships
ufc.tv

Universal Combat Challenge
ucczone.ca/

Web sites

adcombat.com

bjj.prg

extremeselfprotection.com

mmafighter.com

sherdog.com

Index

Mark Hatmaker has 24 years experience in the martial arts (boxing, wrestling, Jiu-jitsu and Muay Thai) including 19 years of instructing. He is a highly regarded coach of professional and amateur fighters, law enforcement officials and security personnel. Mark is founder of Extreme Self Protection (ESP), a research body that compiles, analyzes and teaches the most effective unarmed combat methods known. ESP holds numerous seminars throughout the country each year, including the prestigious Karate College / Martial Arts Universities in Radford, Virginia. He has produced several instructional videos including "Escapes From Impossible Holds" (three volume set), "Ground Zero" (Real World Survival Grappling), "Brutal Submissions" and "Guard Submissions." His first book, *No Holds Barred Fighting*, was published in 2002. He lives in Knoxville, Tennessee.

Doug Werner is the author or co-author of 16 sport and fitness instructional guides including the Start-Up Sports® series. He lives in San Diego, California.